World Stage Press
Verse from the Village

SEASONS OF THE HEART

POEMS BY R. JEROME THOMAS

World Stage Press
Verse from the Village

Seasons of the Heart
© 2022, Robert Jerome Thomas
ISBN: 978-1-952952-29-6

First Edition, 2022

Printed in the United States of America

Proofreading Editing by Sara Khayat
Cover & Layout Design by Lorraine Dean & Krystle May Statler

I dedicate this memoir to my wife, Susan, who has supported me thoroughly in this endeavor. Her love, encouragement and resident critique has allowed peace and motivation on the home front. I am also thankful to my daughters, Alecia, Naivasha, and Kayla during this time of personal growth. Just hearing their voices and listening to their narratives has helped to balance the fluctuations that often exist in the heart of a poet. To my mother, who said, "I was gifted in the area of literary expression" I am truly indebted. Your prayers over my life will live on in the rhythm of these pages. To my siblings, Ronita and Kelesha, I am appreciative of each of your creative works in the world that empowers my desire to contribute to the Thomas children collection.

Finally to the students of the numerous English and Literature classes, where I have been privileged to teach. I thanked the students at Eldoro High School, Taveta, Kenya, who challenged me as we analyzed Chinua Achebe, *Things Fall Apart*. To the students in the Fairfield-Suisun City School District, I am grateful for listening to my daily experimental sonnets. One student was especially moved, that he responded in kind with his own sonnet. I pray that this book will inspire others as it did John Bruni.

In Memoria
Rev. Dr. R. Colby Thomas,
Father Extraordinaire
&
Janvie Carson,
Spiritual Friend/CLI Supporter

CONTENTS

SPRING

SUMMER

AUTUMN

FOREWORD

This book by Rev. Dr. Thomas, is more than a book, it is an offering. It is a gift of what love is, what love can be and how to bring love into one's life. This is an extraordinary book by an extraordinary human being. As a scholar, counselor and minister I am aware of how special Dr. Thomas is and how his hard earned wisdom is presented in this book of poetry. Few people can make claim to having the unique combination of education, service and scholarship as does Dr. Thomas. Those who may have his educational credentials, do not have his outstanding record of service. Those who may have his record of service do not have his educational achievements. The few individuals who may have his educational and service status do not have his national and international experiences from which to draw in writing this poetic work.

I have had the honor of knowing and working with Dr. Thomas during his earlier years. Upon getting reacquainted I was delighted to learn of his spiritual journey which included his works of counseling, prose and poetry. Dr. Thomas's work is replete with sound advice for those who are in crisis situations as well as those who are experiencing the developmental challenges that are a feat of life. The reader will find help for a problem that they are enduring without a sense of being ashamed or misled. They will find assistance for themselves and a resource for others who could use Dr. Thomas's sound guidance. As an act of love I will circulate copies of his published work to family, friends and colleagues.

I am honored to recommend this book as you encounter the various seasons of life. May this book by Rev. Dr. Thomas help you find your Heart.

—Rev. Dr. Don H. Matthews, Ph.D

PREFACE

In honor of one of my spiritual friends, Janvie, who recently transitioned, an alternative title for this collection would be a book of divine loving. The essence of this book has percolated intermittently like a geyser throughout my life. Sacred scripture states, every good and perfect thing that comes from the Father of lights is a gift. This offering is like a papyrus reading for the spiritual aspirant, seek and you will find. Like a piece of black coal, that evidentially turns into a diamond, my life has been one of vertical pressure.

The divine pressure from above was not revealed until my adventures in Kenya, East Africa. Having time to meditate and reflect upon my ancestral heritage in Kenya allowed me to center and ground. The agape love received from the communities where I taught, renewed and restored the unconditional love from above. It was the perfect global location, on the equator, for the turning points in my heart to come into alignment.

As you turn pages of this collection, I hope you will find a line, sonnet, or haiku that will speak to the turning points in your life. I believe each person has entered my path for a divine purpose. Elie Wiesel said, "For the dead and the living, we must bear witness." It has been an honor and privilege to bear witness with others throughout my life, both as a speaker and a listener. One sacred text that continues to resonate in my ear, "Understand this…You must all be quick to listen, slow to speak, and slow to get angry."

Forty years of active listening has left me with a wealth of life changing narratives. I would be an ingrate if I kept these incredible stories to myself. This collection is for the world, including family, loving community, the Veterans and everyone who has sent a prayer for my well-being. I am eternally grateful for this offering, and the prayers that have nurtured every word.

May the revelations continue…

SEASONS OF THE HEART

WINTER

Prayer for Winter

For lo
the winter's past
the rain's over and gone
rebirth moves painfully slow as
ice thaws.

Song of Songs 2:11

Where My Soul Lives!

I live in the land of affirmations
amidst the limitless territory
of bountiful blessings,
I sit on the runway of can-do arrivals
without doubt the deity of God is pressing;
etching through I sense His everlasting arms,
guiding me on Straight Street without alarm.

Goodness and mercy hover overhead,
prompting my heart to receive daily bread;
Illumined by rays reflecting off the seas,
I evolve in the soil of possibilities;
Blessed by beams of solitude,
Joy wakes me each morning as I
sing another song of gratitude;
Kissed by the eternal I journey in
the agape lane of embracing love,
Dipped in divine forgiveness from above.

Pondering theophanies already provided,
Looking forward to running into
epiphanies heavenly guided;
Though dark clouds come and strong winds blow,
These are temporary pauses
preparing me for a supernatural flow;

Sunset's closure will keep me until morning,
anticipating a new dawning;
I rejoice for promises birthed in my spirit,
the revelation knowledge that sits
on full exhibit;
As I to listen to another narrative with
fresh expectation,
I ponder with intention and promising prediction, of
Where my soul lives!

Pursuing Your Dreams

Live the life you've imagined,
Shape it, mold it, let your creative side be fashioned;

Our truest life is when we're in dreams awake,
Pursue them like glistening sun on a lake;

To uncharted waters and undreamed shores,
Portals are waiting to open fastened doors;

Commitment leads to action which brings dreams closer,
Imagination is the touchstone of your character;

Throw your dreams into space like a kite,
You don't know what it will bring back in flight;

A new life, new friend,
new love, a new way to comprehend.

Curly-Head Fred

There is a little boy who likes to play outdoors,
Southern-reared, curious when he explores;
I think I'll not call myself 'boy' anymore,
It's degrading, like being called a whore;
Tender ears should refrain from saying such things,
Worldly knowledge prompts parental butt stings;

Wish I didn't have to experience the things I see,
There must be some reason God has chosen me;
Why must I drink out of 'colored' water fountains
and redirect steps to the 'colored' restroom?
Is this retribution, Lord I still fume!
Got to keep my cool that's what Daddy said,
Don't want to be misconstrued as a hothead;

What's up riding on this divided bus?
Feeling less than, in this segregated fuss,
I want to see the action with the driver,
Money changing, and the protest rider;
Sit back and watch this commotion,
Discourage thoughts about a lynching notion.

Thank God I've got friends
Kenneth, Virgil and Eddie,
Love to shoot marbles with
these three;
We would crawl under houses,
climb oak trees,
These guys were my smartest,
bravest trustees;

Amazing how confident we can feel,
With community, we can face any ordeal;
That's what I miss about those

Louisiana days,
Good trouble on the
dangerous highways;

We looked funny with our big ears
parted hair and spaced teeth,
No one could imagine what
lay underneath;
Our parents had no idea about
our lavish dreams,
They would throw up their hands
if they knew our schemes;

Our desires wasn't anything serious
to worry about,
Nothing crazy that would even cause doubt;
Just wanted a chance to spread wings and fly,
To that majestic playground in the sky!

The Eighth Wonder of the World

Deep within the subconscious of my mind,
A vision continues to rewind;
It stood in the shadows hidden from view,
When you spoke today I had a breakthrough;
It was the loftiest picture imagined,
One filled with insatiable passion;
I saw them as I looked towards the hill,
 A vision of your lips my heart could not be still.

A virtuous set of lips who can find?
Yours might be the next of divine design;
I toured redwoods to view the tallest there,
I heard the giants speak about your lips so fair;
I climbed the Himalayas in the thin air,
Each breeze that swirled whispered of your pair;
I thought Grand Canyon would brighten my day,
Its splendor paled to your twosome archway;

Those succulent plump monuments of bliss,
Very few have been privileged to kiss;
They may be more precious than gold,
Undoubtedly a marvel to behold;
Folks travel to visualize the Empire State's three-sixty,
Makes this globetrotter tear up and misty;

Because I've seen the Taj Mahal,
A fabulous structure of ivory tall;
But the reflection in the pool there,
beckoned me to compare;
At Macchu Picchu, I could not dismiss,
The monks discussing the beauty of your kiss;

I finally made it to the one
who would tell the truth,

Did these lips come from
Moabite Ruth?

Christ the Redeemer welcomed with His arms stretched wide,
He summoned me to sit close by his side;
These lips came from your mother's heart
placed tenderly in her womb,
They were transferred to you
with each step they would perfume;

So glad I've been fortunate to taste the miracle,
Though the touch was years ago;
I replay the image in my dreams,
The sight today made my feelings scream;
That's what happens when your lips are renown,
People search the globe to note what I've found;
The eighth wonder of the world is still in view,
Blessed to adore them once again with you!

Sonnet for Sarah

She entered carrying the world in her hand,
Beauty, structure, wavy, straight
each step seemed intentional but unplanned;
Unassuming was her dress,
Perfectly adorned with emotions waiting to express;

She flexed arms, feet went up and down,
Our heart flowed with each movement
waiting for sundown;
Up went her hair and our spirit went to the sky,
She let it drop and we didn't know how to reply;

But that's how the world makes us feel sometimes,
Mad, sad, glad and afraid
dance brings all that into creative pantomime;
So move Sarah move and never forget,
Every muscle and tendon you must vet;

Until you bring tears to eyes and art to life,
We will encourage your expression
of peace through strife;
Though you exit from this present stage,
May your impact encourage us to engage!

Remnants of Friends Flown Away

Two birds flew pecking on my window sill,
One light with angel lips like down feathers,
The site of their arrival gave me thrill;
Neither could I release from my tether;
The other tall, dark incredibly smart,
Each sang of devotion in the same year,
Unfortunate we lived so far apart;
Their intentions were supremely sincere;
They inched closer especially at night,
The constant racing in my beating chest,
Waiting for just eulogy from their flight;
Tried to be quiet flutter must be addressed,
Each beckoned with their spirited ballet,
My heart said, 'Yes', but wisdom said, 'Delay'!

With a Christmas Heart

The prophet Isaiah prophesied seven centuries ago,
About a Messiah who would bring a divine glow;
A great light in the world for everyone to see,
A radiance to dwell in you and shine in me;

With this light burning bright in our life,
It brings harmony and peace to minimize strife;
No doubt God is with us Immanuel made plain,
Hope is restored which allows us to sustain;

Once again we gather as family and friends,
To renew hope in each other with ways to transcend,
Cherish the wonder of how God sent His Son,
To give us a redemptive plan for everyone;

Take a moment to pause and reflect,
Find novel ways to display inspired intellect;
Appreciate your brother and sister with eyes of glee,
Find non-judgmental ways we all can agree;

Forgiveness is available in small bites or big,
Use the paradigm of Christ that'll never renege.
When we do we may once again reveal,
The supernatural power of love to heal.

Poinsettias Praise

Keep the spirit of Christmas alive,
Paint it with phrases let it revive;
Veins and lifelines reach out to speak,
Wrinkles tell stories with each slanted streak;

Leaf points in variegated ways,
Hopeful promise of future holidays;
Iridescent petals change near light,
Each blade transforming with downward flight;

Arms wide give praise to inner bliss,
Taste red velvet with each bright kiss;
Wish families could mimic fellowship,
Remember feelings from fingertips;

This romantic sea of heart-shaped passion,
Stands as a touchstone of compassion;
Even as red leaves turn green,
With creative views unforeseen;

If this brand whiffed of pine I'd sell this type,
But no fragrance exists when ripe;
No pungent perfume emits from petals,
Not a scent of scarlet from stem metal;

Drooping, ruffled, crinkled down,
So much life as green turns golden brown;
Fifty leaves of hearts waiting to fall,
Feathery creations could blow with a squall;

Should I trash this spurge with seasonal gifts,
Discard it as a periodic shift?
No, like love there can be convergence,
All you need is a pulse of resurgence;

It lingered until early spring,
The other caretaker did the right thing;
Living beyond hope though a cyclic bloom,
Surpassing its stay because love resumed;

Inject the feeling of Christmas morn',
The joy of that day can be reborn;
Lift your heart to a new paradigm,
In the gladness of this pulsating rhyme;

I'll never leave this bundle of love,
As foliage goes to heaven above;
Will keep this image of velvety blaze,
Eternally aglow in poinsettia's praise.

Booster Shots: Extra Dose of the Holy Ghost

Miracle Walking

Sometimes while walking along the path so true,
I see a miracle sign to my breakthrough;

I do not waver or doubt the favor I view,
God said the Holy Spirit would provide an avenue;

So I take another step with blessed assurance,
Believing God has granted a portion of divine insurance;

So if you take your time and look with great intent,
You might walk into a miraculous holy event.

•

Sky on Fire

The sky you see has changed again
to close another day so I pen,
This poem of joy with peaceful bliss
so thankful for the fiery kiss;

I never take any day for granted
Because this might be my last,
I cherish every second
grounded and steadfast;

Before you say sweet dreams tonight to God or your friend,
Be grateful that you took some time to mindfully apprehend.

•

Tricubes

Love Your Liver

Healthy weight
Balanced meal
Exercise

No toxins
Olive oil
Enemas

Wheatgrass fast
Broccoli
Eat walnuts

•

Capitol Security Failure

Derelict
Calculate
Delinquent

Domestic
Terrorist
Protocol

Disregard
Failure of
Leadership

•

The Gravity of Coddling Killers

A bad day
Poor excuse
Privileged

Tragedy
Police fail
Acts must stop

Heavy heart
Bereavement
Can't come back.

•

She Said

Didn't want
To be just
One more girl

Couldn't do
Casual
Sex with me.

No commit
And so she
Let me go.

•

He Said, 40 years later

Bye Sweetness
Did not have
A real choice

She remained
In my mind
Question mark

Finally
Got resolve
Took too long!

•

A Solstice Tricube

Winter start
Solstice here
Bringing light

Special note
Planets meet
Christmas star

Shortest day
Make it last
Auspicious!

•

Don't Sit There

The pressure
Of the bed
Is easy

If you stay
But if you
Decide to

Get up be
Ready to
Work your butt!

•

One Button Change

TV is
Addictive
Because you

Don't have to
Move muscle
Stories change

Emotions
And you are
Forever changed!

•

Artist-Heart Brain

Fill the well
involves the
active search

Of pictures
refreshing
reservoirs

Art is born
Attention
springing forth!

•

Midnight Blues

Discouraged by life there
are times my vessel is
depleted and I want to die.

In those moments
when the tank is nearly drained,
delirious thoughts flow.

At midnight on this Oahu beach
I hear a thousand roosters crow
canceling the sound of ocean waves,

Placing headphones over ear plugs, I ask
come sweet sleep and escort tinnitus away
putting thoughts of sabotage to rest,

When sleep deprivation is endless,
like Niagara Falls I want to pull
the plug and end it all.

When the HVAC won't cut off
and partner's snoring never ends
I want to push pause and escape.

Demented thoughts fill the tenth floor
though tempting I dare not step
beyond that open doorway,

It would be too easy to take a leap,
and prove what they always
said, "I knew he was crazy!"

but that is not my legacy.
Can't let my kids grieve for eternity,

because they'd never know why
or allow my wife to wonder,
 "What did I do?"
Though enticing, I keep myself
from the sliding door, knowing
that path would be painful.

Finally, dawn comes through the crucible of despair
lifting the veil leading to the warm green light
where I'm comforted by blankets of love.

I write because nothing has been easy.
It's not easy now. But that's ok because
I am alive and this is the breakthrough.

I write for all the unhinged souls
who needed one more hour of sleep
before they passed through sanctuary's door.

For the storytellers with unbearable pain, I live.
For those with PTSD who couldn't help themselves, I live.
For the bridge jumper, mainliner and over the cliff seekers, I live.
For those who never had a voice because the hurt
was overwhelming, I live.

New Year

Fresh beginnings birth
Seed moments in heart of faith
First step of staircase

Nothing predestined
Past obstacles become the
Gateways to new start

Valentine Dream

I too dream,
that one day every sunbeam you
feel will remind you of the rays of love
perpetually emitting from my heart;

That the breath you are breathing is
the exhale of love that has
filled up the room, the house and the
atmosphere with a romantic aroma;

I have a dream that every waking
moment is filled with angelic thoughts
of heaven right here on Earth;

I have a dream that the ship you have been
waiting for has already come, so get
on board, taste and see that the Lord is good
and my love is sweeter than honey in the honeycomb;

From the crown of your head to the toes of your feet;

I have a dream that you live in the
vortex of an all-knowing, all-wise ever present love;
That guides, keeps and propels us
to a state of euphoric bliss;

Yes, I too dream.

Ode to Unadulterated Love

Only because we know each other in spirit
can this immaculate love exist,
This essence and passion I can't resist;
my love is beyond eros that would taint it,
Beyond phileo that would dilute it;
So it dwells in the sphere of agape,
Gathering nectar from Yahweh's bouquet.

Even syllabic expressions miss the mark,
But that is why I must embark,
To explain the fervor that I feel,
When you sit close, my heart must not conceal;

Your aura emits electrical charges,
"You must be hooked up to a generator!"
Your vibrational chakras are so strong,
I might need a respirator;
So I can catch my, my breath, from this wave of emotions,
Drop me in the ocean so I can cool from these palpitations;
What's going on can't be denied,
There's a fire burning inside;
Something occurs playing on this keyboard,
Every note that we strike seems right
for in God there is no discord;

I really need to bring this to a close,
With the Lord being our helper who knows;
Remain open to every possibility,
There is awesome opportunity,
It's grand to wake each morning with a kind thought,
Wonderfully simmering in the oven of forethought;

For we are His workmanship created unto good works,
Not ashamed of the gospel which is a perk;

To raise each day with healing in our wings,
And lift up our voices it compels one to sing;
Praise to the Lord the Almighty reigns,
Hallelujah to God our eternal King!

One Word from You

One Word from you is,
Like a rainbow after a downpour,
Like a dove flying over a tranquil sky,
Like a phone call you've been waiting for,
Like a triple-berry pie.

One word from you is,
Like heat flowing through cold vents to defrost cold feet,
Like lentil soup teeming with bay leaves and bulgur wheat,
Like sunflowers awaiting relief from a butterfly,
Like ladybugs lingering for the wind to soar high.

One word from you is,
Like Longfellow conversing with Thoreau,
Like Hugo sipping tea with Poe,
Like Hemingway opening the door for Dickinson,
Like May talking beauty with Emerson.

One word from you is,
Like dewdrops on morning glories waiting to surprise,
Like hands on little faces opening baby eyes;
Like fragrance from a rose that lifts you from your knees,
Like stars lighting the skies, that helps you find your keys.

One word from you is,
Like powdery snowflakes falling gently on green grass,
Like rushing waters cascading pass;
Like snow melting slowly on top of Kilimanjaro,
Like a nightingale singing waiting for tomorrow.

One word from you is,
Like pulsations from your heart to mine,
sending quivers up my spine,
Like nerve messages stopping to pause
for this immediate cause,

Like Canadian geese flying in a V headed north,
Like fireworks exploding perfectly on July Fourth,

One word from you,
Makes everything complete,
So I'll take my seat!

Now We Heal

Now we start the process, now we start the decree,
From a place of agony to a place of walking free;
This walk will impact the essence of our inside,
Our heart even the tears we have cried;

We'll learn resilience of fighting in the pit,
Dispelling darts and arrows, dealing with hypocrites;
Through it all we'll become focused and succinct,
Find ways to connect our causes and truly link;

I believe in the human spirit especially in defeat,
The ability to rise from ashes in the midst of the heat;
Grieve if you must take a nap from all the stress,
Then wake up determined ready to address;

Tell the truth by your actions, be genuine in your speech,
Teach your children, and be available to preach;
We'll survive my friends if we walk together,
We've proved we can handle any weather!

Train Up a Child

After church today, I spoke to an 8-year-old blond freckled young boy who had a basketball in his hand. He was with his parents about to eat lunch. I said, "looks like you're starting early like Steph Curry." To my surprise the boy said, he hated Steph Curry. I said to him, "what about forgiveness?"

His parents said, "We just came from church, and he hates Curry because he asked, but didn't get an autograph from him." The parents said, "He'll get over it." Though it happened months ago, the boy still holds that 'hatred' in his heart.

It's up to parents to realize that little hurts and hates manifest into larger degrees of animosity. Little pricks of dislike unchecked grow into cysts of contempt.

Parents it's up to you to keep the dialogue going. Never let hate fester, you never know the long-term effect.

The Patient's Hope

Deep within the bowel,
The tumor grows within,
Waiting for a vowel.

She throws in the towel,
Unsure of the root cause,
Deep within the bowel.

Cat smells minuscule bowel,
Poking, pawing, pancreas,
Deep within the bowel.

Doctor has avowal,
Giving remedy repair,
Deep within the bowel.

Peptide is the dowel,
Antidote for cancer,
Waiting for a vowel.

Exam will clarify
Answer, asymptomatic,
Deep within the bowel,
Waiting for a vowel!

Rose-colored Deceit

Said on January twenty-secondth
"We have it under control,"
Only one case reported
so the government had no goal;
On February tenth, no goal shot up to eleven,
Forty-five and Pence said,
"It'll be gone by the end of April's
raindrops from heaven."

On February twenty-sixth with fifty-seven cases
Somebody wanted to be a hero,
Leadership swayed, "within a couple days
we'll be close to zero."
Next day was unbelievably satirical,
When CIC said, "Coronavirus will
disappear like a miracle."

On February twenty-eighth
they politicized as the numbers grew to sixty,
Republicans said, "The virus is the
Democrats "new hoax theory."
On March fourth as the cases doubled
they reported deaths of eleven,
Leadership told a white lie, "people recover
by going to work 24/7."

Sheep of Another Fold

Trapped by the church
with parental aspiration,
I came forth ambushed,
with no choice.

Instructions received in utero
said sanctuary was the cycle,
Worship like the morning sun,
with firmament above, ocean below.

Prayer like water rising,
Faith like clouds condensing,
Spirit like precipitation falling,
I could not stop this natural order.

So I hunkered down, shut up
reverent, humble, obedient,
appreciative of food and shelter
grateful to be alive.

But the pain of disorder called,
Needing to understand discord,
Longing to experience mess,
I plunged into turbulence on purpose.

To flow with the worship of
worldliness, the song of unrest,
The testimony of turmoil,
The god of godlessness.

Did I learn anything from this
dive? Yes, there is credo in no
creed, Free spirit has form,
No spiritual base has foundation,

Call it ambiguous,
Nebulous,
Perplexing
or Problematic,

This is the sheepfold I inherited,
So I listen and let feel,
The mud and shadows,
The dark and cloudy,
Having empathy to understand the mystery!

It's ok, not being understood

Sometimes I have to start with the premise,
people don't understand me.
Unable to discern my rhyme and reasons,

They can't comprehend my midnight birth,
born in segregation,
weaned in discrimination
reared in revelation.

Don't understand the silence in my spirit,
The words that beg to be pulled out of my heart,
The truth that yearns to be extracted from my gut.

They're unable to grasp the struggles
or get tired of listening.
Well, you may be tired but I'm just getting started.

And you will listen,
Because I have bled, clawed, and scratched
through layers of ridicule.

Through pebbles, earthworms and nematodes,
I've inched through the bedrock of neglect,
to lift from the pit of silence.

From the grave where no one hears
your words, I speak.
From the mineral salts that have
penetrated the substrata, I speak.

Small but mighty, weaving myself
through centuries of being stepped on,
plowed under and rototilled, I speak.

With the natural determination
of every seed
that has shaken the dust, I speak.

Subtle but profound, for the voices silenced
in the womb,
because they had no power, I speak.

For the babies who died in the crib, I speak.
For children who are seen but not heard, I speak.
For the scorned or despised, I speak

For those who may never be understood,
because no one took the time.
It's ok!

Exquisite

To glance upon her frame, is like beholding the sun,
Inspires every fiber, so blessed to be the one;
With grace and flow, she skates across a lake,
If she ever chose a partner, I'ld gladly partake;

Her caring hands, delicately woven with love,
Pure landscape of handiwork from above;
Some call her different, others unique,
Hope you live long to gaze upon her mystique;

Heed her story and read between the lines,
Spot resilience lovingly inclined;
Narrative complex, like wells filled with bold,
More better than diamonds, more costly than gold;

Glad to be given the charge, of this easy chore,
of tellling about a queen that also adores;
Not sure why mist falls from her tender eyes,
Moistens flowers providing food for butterflies;

Carbon cut with precision over time,
Manicured contours loveliness sublime;
Soul of Nefertiti and Venus combined,
Unequivocally blessed by the divine.

My Wells are Full

Vulnerable is my heart tonight,
I want to remove every slight;

So I forgive everyone who sent
a Dear John letter,
It was probably for the better;

I pardon any who abandoned the ship,
Leaving me on an island
in the middle of a friendship;

To anyone where I have done the same,
I feel like Zacchaeus so it's time to reclaim;

Please excuse if I talked too much
that wasn't my intent,
Sometimes I get carried away when I vent;

Forgive me if I bruised your inner soul,
Please release me from parole;

My wells are teeming by the grace of the Lord,
Time to pick up every voyager
who slipped overboard;

Let's lay aside every weight that does
so easily beset,
And run with patience
the race without regret;

This is my plea though it be simple and plain,
It's high time to wipe the slate clean;

Let the Lord abundantly pardon and reign,
When we do we might regain;

The peace and joy we once held dear,
Let's take this agape love to a higher sphere!

SPRING

Prayer for Spring

Truth shall
Spring from the earth,
Seeds of new beginnings
Promises hope of fresh
blossoming with joy.

Ps. 85:11

When Grown Men Cry

There is something cathartic when men cry,
It's a rare scene when tears fall from their eyes;
Because it comes from an ultra-deep place,
It appears to contort or change their face;
Saw Dad's tears as he sang the post-sermon's plea,
Changed world view of what male tears meant to me;

When men, grown men actually let it flow,
These are not croc' tears for a phony show;
Neither saline leaks from a movie ending,
Nor moisture runs from a marriage pending;
No sobs for the old lady's retreat home,
Or some drone returning to the honeycomb;

It's because care flowed from an unknown hoot,
A human laid down their normal pursuit;
Brought Esau and Jacob's fighting to halt,
As Joseph told his kin it's no one fault;
They reached with heart in hand, and said
"Don't shoot this one deserves a second chance."

When men muse on that dawn a light comes on,
As they reflect on the phenomenon;
And they cannot help but well-up inside,
Grateful a companion was there to guide;
That's all one person wants from another,
Consideration from the Band of Brothers.

Social Justice, Senryu

Twenty first century
I'm still appalled when referred
to as "you people"

On elevator
white woman shuts purse tighter
as if I need it

The Nile still runs deep
in those who can't adjust fact
Ancient blacks were there

Eyes may never see
Colorblind ideology
But we live the pain

They tried to erase
Culture history genius
Truth will always raise

Empty stomachs need
willing hands to feed plenty
from gracious hearts

Wicked empowers
Removing filters of love
Healing is needed

You have two choices
Why take path of Jericho
Choose Golgotha's way!

Waiting for Another One!

Hopes and dreams are thoughts that come to mind,
Words that ring since the Warriors last shined;
Forty years back, missed the team of my youth,
By taking a Peace Corps journey to
Kenya to find my truth;
I missed Attles' passes and Barry's free throws,
The smooth touch of Wilkes,
Thurmond's dunks and elbows;
They rose to the top in season of '75,
through the injuries they survived;

Now, I'm privileged to be alive,
Thousands have waited for this day to arrive;
Proud to don Warriors blue and gold wear,
People can't help to stop and stare;
Fans have been in expectancy a lifetime,
To see Curry's threes and turn on a dime;
My brother Clay can hit a streak,
Splash brothers prepared to show their mystique;

Yes, time for Draymond and Barnes to get their just due,
showcase their skills with Bogut too;
Iguodala and Speights are superb when they play,
Lee and Ezeli can move on this hardwood canopy;
Pray for Coach Kerr's leadership, who knows how to win,
For guidance as they show a new kind of discipline;

May hearts stay focused on the game that brings us together,
With appreciation sustain us through playoff weather;
Let's use this same excitement in our daily lives,
Stay positive and we'll rewrite narratives;
Peace to my brothers and sisters everywhere,
Time to win another for 'The City' where I was
conceived is my earnest prayer.

Revenge of the Nice Guys

With all the awful news,
about the less than nice guy blues;
I think it's proper time,
to reprise an old paradigm;

Nice guys is a tired thought to some degree,
Women say, "He's nice" but girl "Not for me;"
Some knew a nice guy kind, warm, respectful,
Super sensitive, never neglectful;
Thought he'd be nerdy, weak, bland, boring,
But they were impressed by his outpouring.

If women want commitment
and long-term relationship,
why do they keep sacrificing niceness
for Mister Hip?
Sounds like niceness is never quite enough,
Though women won't say it publicly
they appear to want gorilla-tough;

Two marriages showed me nice guys are
old-fashioned, some want the jerk,
There's cred in being with a bad scout
who's a piece of work;
Many women would rather fall,
For the bad boy who hasn't called;
Than the nice guy who texted you twice this week,
And filled your inbox with a tender tweet;

Nice guys are too nice
because they don't offer women the chase,
Abuse has created a strange interface;
Women are wired for complicated
which leaves the nice guy in the dust,

Only way to get out of the friend zone
is to readjust;

Nice guys have to realize
Some may not appreciate kindness in their face,
Until they see deception in its place.

They often have to get their hearts broken
once, twice or maybe three times,
Before realizing
they need a new paradigm.

Poems of Redemption

Beauty in the Eyes of the Beholder

I do not love you like a marble bust, with skin
as pale as Chinese takeout cartons, with no upper lip.
I love you like black things are to be loved; with earnestness,
whose finality is truth.

I love you like the backside of God, the good face that must
be sought after, but never revealed; thanks to your love, I
realize black is the essence from which all color comes.

I love you without knowing the bones of human civilization,
I love you directly, grasping there is no variance of beauty;
where shade and length of hair has no discrimination.

Forgive, if I have strayed from reality, pray when I stand
before the Creator, the radiance of your inward nature will
be affirmed afresh without comparison!

•

Cherish, a Forgotten Grace

From the beginning God stepped out on love,
Giving us the gift to hear from above;
Formed in the likeness of Almighty God,
With thanksgiving responders to applaud;

Lifting the Father, Son and Holy Ghost,
Let's raise cups to give our sisters a toast;
We must reverse the negative vibe,
Degradation talk I will not subscribe;

Where are the days when we cherished women?

When we couldn't wait to see them again;
When we were not afraid to call them dear,
Admired and sometimes shared a tear;
Nobody could truly love us
unconditionally in the midst of our demise,
So it's time my sisters to revise;
Let me take time to wash the slate clean,
The sensations that made you feel less than pristine;

Forgive me when I did not give you props
You deserved to be hailed from the treetops;
You merit an Oscar award,
for holding us like a three-fold cord;

Time to rewrite the script
and burn those derogatory remarks,
Time to set off a revolution
that heals and creates sparks;
Let's create a redemptive renaissance,
One that causes a voluntary response;

A period that brings black men
to their knees in repentance,
An era that accentuates
interdependence;
For we can never be what we were called
to be unless we cherish our sisters,
They need to be embraced and valued
as co-creators;

I will do my part by spreading the news,
Think before you speak and lift up endearing views;
With prayer, we can make breakthroughs,
And change the course of history with positive reviews;

Redemption is at the heart of God's supernatural plan,
It is meant for every woman and man;

We have a biblical mandate to reclaim restore and anoint,
Let us walk from this day forward and never disappoint!

•

Passion, Need I Say More

You lost the passion you once had,
It left the moment I said, "Yes"
You seem impatient to move on,
The embers of fire have grown cold.

Is the carnal conquest over,
since I have been royally licked?
Don't be fooled by media's rage,
It takes more to keep me ablaze,

Hugs, kisses, gentle PDA,
A foot massage and bubble bath,
The person that caused your first view,
Is marveled what's in your playbook.

You can run to my Sierras,
They are majestic and superb,
You can dip in my warm Cabo
and smooth groove in my Yucatan,

Barbados is hot this season,
Whisper sweet nothings in my ear,
Tell me you decadent dessert,
Your plan on this body of bliss,

I'm a wick waiting to be lit,
I'll give keys, with free pass permit;
Light the candle, let it burn slow,
We're going to a new plateau!

•

Soft, But Oh So Strong

In the midst of being a strong, black woman
like Harriet Tubman and Sojourner Truth,
Sometimes I succumb to the little things
like soft touches and Baby Ruths;
I wish I didn't have to be strong, it's stressful you know,
But somebody has to carry the load through the woe;
I accept the role that was handed down by my mother,
When I reflect upon my life I wouldn't have it any other;
Sometimes I would love to get off this merry-go-round,
That's why I need a wise black man to keep me sound;

I see him in the morning, feel him in the afternoon,
Can't wait to view his face underneath this silver moon;
Sometimes I want to feel vulnerable, naked on a limb,
So he can catch me if I have to swim;

It's liberating and freeing, weak and sometimes strong;
In the arms of my black brother I am lifted by his song;
It might be ain't no woman like the one I got,
To make me happy doesn't take a lot;
Or night and day, you are the one,
Only you beneath the moon and under the sun;
Whether near to me or far,
It's no matter baby, where you are,
I think of you, night and day.

My lover and my friend has the capacity,
To love me with a unique audacity;
Ladies take a tip from me and listen up,
That special man is waiting to fill your cup;
Take your time and hold his hand,
Let him know he is a tender perceptive man;
Made just for you for such a time as this,
Don't forget to lean over gently, seal the moment with a kiss!

•

Soft is All I Desire!

If I told you that I need soft
would that be so hard,
Just a little consideration,
please listen to my regard;
Get off that uneven spot
that's abrasively coarse,
Come over here to the smooth
and agreeable source;

Don't do well on tough surfaces
and concrete seats,
I'd live totally
if provided a comfy retreat;
No need to be rough
I'm not one of the guys,
All I ask is your yielded touch
willing to harmonize;

Lower the music
subdued and cool,
Keep the vibration gentle
like an infinity pool;
Don't need loud colors
to arouse my visual field,
Just fluid pastels to soften
this garden of appeal;

Callous or sharp words
never helped me learn one bit,
But if you give me silky outlines
I will truly commit;
Something about tender
sends shivers up my spine,
I'm a lady that has been
uniquely designed;

I've paid my dues to be
pampered with fur,
Delicate flower petals would be nice
velvet I prefer;
Be patient with this feeling
that is hypnotically serene,
Shower me with feathers,
spoil me like a queen!

•

The Finesse of Assertiveness

There is a fine line between strong-willed,
self-assured versus demanding and domineering,
This thin line is so slender that if you breathe hard
it will bend her;
Bends towards pushy, bends towards loud,
Bends towards the offensive that is often allowed;

Who is to say what is the reason?,
Is it because there are not enough black men
or did someone create this treason?;
I think it is a conspiracy to create confusion,
No one sane would concoct this contusion;

Black women call it assertiveness, black men call it bossy,
Whatever this filet gumbo is, it's cayenne saucy;
Black men resist the tinge of bossiness which brings
back traumatic memories,
When all we needed was a hug not a lecture of miseries;

We understand your need black women for independence,
For that same drive runs through our transcendence;
But we do not need another mother nor you a father,
What we need is to understand each other;
We didn't create this scarcity or family adversity,
These capitalist variables were thrust upon us with duplicity;

But we can work this out when we comprehend,
We've been dealt a painful hand.
I'm sorry for the brothers who harbor a resentful grudge,
They are still working on their anger and sludge;
Some of this displeasure is not because of you,
It's challenging to forget injury when the mind
wanders in review;

I pray for the day when black men can take the lead,
And women will feel trusting enough to heed;
A time when this fine line will not be cancerous but benign,
A season of diplomacy and caring skill,
A time when our dialogue will fulfill.

•

The Power of Embrace

When arms reach around the soul of another
Who knows the power of a hug,
The strength of warm acceptance
Brings redemption in a pleasant tug.

Each resolves questions about the last touch,
A hug creates a scab which is never too much.
Eight hours without a hug can seem like an eternity,
the stillness of the night may not bring clarity.

The stars look pretty but they cannot embrace,
the moon illuminates but it cannot replace;
the lovingkindness of subtle grace,
the tenderness around our heart space.

That is what a hug can do,
bring relief if genuine and true;
the longer and more intense the bliss,
made special when sealed by a kiss.

Response to Mentors: Poetic Seed

First time I heard the ancient rivers speak,
Was in a room of musical critique;
Truth resounded like a shaman's singing bowl,
As elder Gil put blues to Langston's scroll;

Notes jumped off the page with prophetic form,
Sweat equity brought this bard to perform;
Met and interviewed this living icon,
Whose radical became my lexicon;

Hughes and Scott-Heron overhauled my soul,
Sounds of jazz poetry transformed earth's goal;
Serpentine shapes of rhythm coiled in my mind,
Spent life-time unwinding its design;

Realized waves of this poetic ocean,
Urged excavation for deep emotion;
Like a diver unhappy with last plunge,
I dove in searching like a greedy sponge;

Trekked to Africa discerning native home,
Explored ancient rivers as I roamed;
Seed was planted Harlem Renaissance of old
versed by Black Renaissance of new,
This neophyte desiring to embody the two!

Kelesha Flows (aka K)

Like water rushing down a mighty stream,
Like rain splashing down a hilly ravine,

Like Jordan in the zone and Tiger in the flow,
Like a Ferrari hum or BMW dynamo,
K flows

Like morning glory opening to dawn,
Spirit opens a seam in K's chiffon,
Unveiling notes of recognition,
Sovereign hand of smooth rendition,

So flow with rich tones of harmonic blend,
Flow with cool rhymes of fluid descend,
Flow with feeling and finesse,
Flow with abundant confidence,

Flow with melodic composition,
Flow with pulsating syncopation,
Flow with shifting vibrato and sound,
Flow where percussive tempo abounds;

Even when there's no epiphanal call,
Even when the tidal waves are small,
Even when the inspiration is not there,
Even when the volcanic lava is rare,

Even when the flow is gentle and petite,
And the waterfall becomes obsolete,
K Flows!

My Mom Loved Sports

I wonder how life would have been
if I knew Mom loved sports as she does,
I think it's an affinity that
gives my heart pause;

I wonder how many times she went
to the ballpark to see,
Her father Walter and my Uncle,
lovingly called Ba-by;

Her cheers and the fears,
the heartache and the tears;
The agony of defeat,
and the joy of victory;

I have only grown to appreciate
my Mom's joy to spectate,

So now I understand the game
is one thing she holds dear,
So I hold this austere moment
with a different type of sincere.

Go watch a game with your loved ones today,
and maybe you'll be blessed with an
appreciative heartfelt bouquet.

Spiritual Haikus

Channel One

Benefit blessing
The right of divine healing
Entitled by grace

When sickness enters
Start quoting healing scripture
Word declares soundness

Power of the tongue
Can bring death or life if used
Exercise your gift

We're blessed in the fields
Blessed from the east to the west
Redeemed from the pit

No bad news despair
Friend sticks closer than brother
Love tender mercies

Enemy afraid
Of exposure, fearful of
Light power in you

•

Channel Two

Give God best time first
And your efforts will be blessed
With more time given

Seek My direct ways
Do not run ahead of Me
　　Let Me lead and guide

　　When you love someone
You desire to share everything
　　You go to them first

　　If you seek Me, I
Will release an anointing
　　To understand My Word

　　Winds and storm may rage
Keep your eyes and heart rooted
　　And you won't be moved

　　By waiting and by
calm you shall be saved in quiet
　　Through trust your strength lies!

•

Channel Three

　　Give thanks to the Lord
Proclaim His greatness. Let the
　　whole world know His works

　　Come, Holy Spirit
Ignite within, the living
　　flame of awesome love

　　Be merry and glad
brother was dead, is alive
　　was lost and now found

　　Remember wonders,
miracles He has performed
　　Search for the Lord's strength

Embrace Your Mountain

If you don't spend time with the Lord,
You won't spend time for the Lord.
Some say if you're so heavenly minded that you're no earthly good.
Yet many are so earthly minded that they are no heavenly good.

The Fragrance of a Rose

The disciples were absorbed in a discussion of Lao Tzu's dictum:

Those who know do not say; those who say do not know. When the Master entered they asked him what the words meant. Said the Master, "Which of you knows the fragrance of a rose?" All of them knew. Then he said, "Put it into words." All of them were silent.

Seating in my swing, I contemplate how fortunate I am to have a front porch,
My vision touches the beauty of what only the eyes can see,
Lilac amethyst sit on my breakfast nook waiting for a breeze,
Morning glories arch their tender necks soaking every beam of sunshine,
Marigolds peek out from their earthly dwelling,
To let world know red and yellow hues will not be denied,
Gardenias sit in ivory clusters waiting to be plucked,
Realizing their existence depends on the gardener's care;
And my roses I love them tenderly,
Like my father taught me on a foggy Oakland morning,
Even without care, they attract nature's best,
Bees fly to taste the sweet nectar,
While the wind kisses loose leaves on moist grass,
I know the fragrance of a rose, strong yet slight,
Temporary but eternal,
A scent for the ages but also right now,
I take a deep breath inhaling God's creation,
With gratitude exhaling the blessing of His handiwork.

The Color of Trauma

I remember the first time
I got stopped on Saturday,
spring of '70 on Shattuck.

Driving Dad's gold Nova station wagon,
was a teenager's dream,
Fatherly trust of traveling on these
streets of protest, magical.

Before I was confronted by the "pigs" in blue,
didn't know what to do,

White CHP fellow walked up on my left
tapping on glass ready to draw,
"License, registration."

License in hand, registration
on visor in clear view, he asked,
"What are you carrying back there?"
I said, "nothing sir."

City of Berkeley backup pulled up
behind and I heard shotguns racked,
I exited as they searched the cargo floor,
Not sure what they were looking for.

Police posse didn't know my Boy Scouts troop,
met in Oakland's Saint Augustine Church,
where Black Panther Party kept their guns,
and funeralized their members.

Did their computer find out my father,
Worked with Martin Luther King, Jr. in Mississippi,
Intimidated by KKK cross burning in Shreveport.

I matched the profile,
Six feet one ectomorph huge Afro
Adolescent facial hair big smile
With no explanation, I was monitored
for one hour like a blackbird,
but I could not hide, and I dare not
make a sound as I set between
crosshairs expecting to shed red,

like they did on
Mark Clark,
Bobby Hutton,
Fred Hampton.

I was a statistic waiting to happen.

But the storm never came
my day of departure
had not come,

As I prayed
angels appeared and
placed a shroud over
bloodthirsty hearts.

Without a word garrison blue left,
shotguns cocked,
orange sirens blazing.

To assault
another big-haired brother
that matched the profile
of a Panther sympathizer.

I never drove that gold
Nova again.
That trauma had come
and gone.

After the eighteenth time
with no Afro,
I still live with the cardiac
of driving while black.

Bring Back Gordon

To remind us of
keloid scars
of battle for liberty,
birthmarks of emancipation
that will never heal.

To prick our selective amnesia
show us Whipped Peter,
Your spider-webbed back
haunts our moral conscience.

Take off your shirt
and expose again
the abuses of slavery.

Unveil the tender wound of bigotry,
where hydrogen peroxide
cannot assuage the cancer
of intolerance.

Though we pour libations
on your wound, no antiseptic
can mend the deceitful lash of hate.

With every singe of injustice,
scabs are torn from skin
without mercy.

Try not to be traumatized
by the temporary redness
turning brown, delicate aches
will soon return.
When you hear the police siren,
and see paramedic warning
lights,

Remember the picture of Gordon.

As long as
advancement is stopped,
Discrimination is pervasive,
opportunity limited,
Vacancy closed.

Raw skin still tender
Tender skin still raw.

Fight the Good Fight of Faith, *1 Timothy 6:12*
Songwriting–Rap

Verse One
This is C.T., don't give the glory to me,
'Cuz there's a fellow, they call Him J.C.

Now there's a battle going on, across the land,
Some say that we'll die by the stroke of a hand,

Sisters killing sisters, brother killing brothers,
Nation killing nation, without retaliation.

Chorus
That the real war is not against flesh and blood,
Or the boys and the girls in the hood,

The real war is for bodies and souls,
Of men and women, no matter how old.

With mercy on your left and goodness on your right,
Fight the good fight of Faith, with all your might.

Verse Two
Temptation might say, "Change a rock to bread"
But you tell Satan, "Get out-of-a my head."

'Cuz "Man shall not live by bread alone"
But by every word of God's Megaphone

God shouts through His Word, which is the light,
Be strong in the Lord, and-the-power-of-His-might

Verse Three
Now a good soldier, never goes to battle unprepared
So raise your weapon, high in the air,

Hold your ground, when you're under attack,
Let the angels fight your battle, and cover your back,

The angel of the Lord camps round about,
And one day, "The Lord will descend with a shout"

Chorus

With mercy on your left, and goodness on your right,
Fight the good fight of faith with all your might,

Fight, fight the power,

'Cuz He's the Alpha, Omega
beginning and end
born to save a world so deep in sin

I say fight, fight the power

Keep fighting, raise your weapon
Keep praying, keep fighting!

Rodriguez High Challenge
Songwriting–Rap

Intro
What up, mustangs, time to challenge your view
And look at the world with the goals you pursue,

Chorus
Regardless of what, your friends or parents say,
You are somebody, with a duty today;
So I charge you this moment
admonish you now,
Don't let anybody, determine your Wow;

Verse One
Because-one-day Mom said, "I'd never finish tenth grade
In my early years, she was throwing some shade."
Dad said, "I was useless, could always-be-a-pimp,
but that didn't help my emotional limp."

Verse Two
Because I've got mountains to climb and countries to cross,
One day, somebody is gonna call me a boss;
When the roll is called and the muster is taken,
I'll tell the story everyone was mistaken;

Chorus

Verse Three
Now, I hope you're listening and take this sonnet to heart,
Once you go down the wrong path, it's hard to restart;
Take-it from-this-OG, and avoid the pain,
No one knows the catalyst, inside your brain;

Tag
So I charge you this moment
admonish you now,
Don't let anybody, determine your Wow;
Right now, determine your Wow,
In your heart, make a vow,
In your mind you're make it somehow,

Through the fire,

With great desire,

Inner love'll take you higher!

Tag

Not your friends,
Not your parents,
Your inner child,
Be reconciled,

Through the Fire!

The Sweet Spot

Second time this week
patient shared
No reason to
live.

All attempts to
assimilate
back to society
failed.

Job interviews
housing issues
all fell through the
cracks.

Recurring nightmares of
putting
   bombs on
     planes
that killed people will not
leave.

One word,
One phrase,
One miscue,
could send this patient
into a
tailspin.

Prayed for wisdom
discussed traumatized brain
is bottom-heavy,
primal areas high,
cognitive areas low

amygdala disconnected
in overdrive.

Suddenly wonder flashed
through this dimly lit room,
sunshine parted
the mental skies,
Patient's thousand-yard stare
recalibrated, looked at me
and said
"Finally somebody understands."

I sat in silence, thankful for
this moment of clarity
when hopelessness turns
to hope,
sadness finds a sparkle
to sustain the day.

Golfers, tennis and baseball
players have a name for this
miracle,
when everything changes
dialogue happens and
healing transpires,
they call it
the sweet spot.

ABC's of Godly Identity

When people ask me how I'm doing, I respond with a Godly Truth, versus the worldly lie by telling the inquirer, I'm...

Too Anointed to be Disappointed...
Too Blessed to be Stressed...
Too Consecrated to be Agitated...

Too Dedicated to be Fabricated...
Too Edified to be Crucified...
Too Forgiven to be Backslidden...

Too Glad to be Mad...
Too Healed to be Concealed...
Too Inspired to be Tired...

Too Justified to be Nullified...
Too Kept to be Inept...
Too Lifted to be Downshifted...

Too Manifested to be Detested...
Too Northward to be Downward...
Too Ordained to be Profaned...

Too Proficient to be Deficient...
Too Quickened to be Sickened...
Too Redeemed to be Declaimed...

Too Sanctified to be Mortified...
Too Transformed to be Conformed to this world...

Too United to be Divided...
Too Victorious to be Notorious
Too Wonderfully-Made to be Dismayed...

Too eXhilirated to be Humiliated...
Too Yielded to be Dismissed..
Too Zealous to be Jealous...

SUMMER

Prayer for Summer

Summer
Is near when branch
becomes tender showing
leaves, awakening fire within
belly.

Matthew 24:32

Today, I Cried

I almost cried at my sister's birth what a wonder to behold,
I should have cried when I left my childhood friends cold;

I thought about releasing a tear when JFK won,
I came close when that Navy LT left his son,

MLK's death brought tears to a nation's eyes,
My aqueduct could not squeeze a drop for the dreamer's demise;

But something happened when parents asked me to bring home friends,
They had no idea of the racial dilemma that caused my heart to pretend;

In Louisiana my parents said, "Stay away from whites."
In California they changed, "Stand clear of blacks."

I wanted Niagara Falls to flow when black girlfriend said, "stop,"
I was so enamored with Nefertiti's blackness I turned into a sop;

I needed to cry and figure out what caused this and why,
My disconnected heart ran through relationships like a drive-by;

The stress of trying to fit in,
Between whitey's group with this fair skin;

The pressure of being the invisible man,
When I tried to obey the oppressor's plan;

I shunned what caused others to succumb,
Today, I cried when I realized what I had become.

Juneteenth Ethic

Let us never forget this day,
The reason why they made it a holiday;
It was emancipation from slavery,
Freedom from everything unsavory;
That made servitude inhuman and callous,
Let us never forget this heartless malice;

Feels like the present rule is trying to take us back,
Because of the ugly ways of a megalomaniac;
Do not let this day go by,
Take a moment and personally identify;
Think about your response to keep freedom true,
Think about what your ancestors went through;

No more beatings, lynchings or running to get free,
No more fighting, because somebody treats you like a nobody;
No more separation of husband and wife,
No more family splitting that causes strife;
We must stand up and tell others enslavement is done,
For any and everyone;

Do your part and set the captives free,
Start with self and clean up personal debris;
Clear out the clutter, break the chains that bind,
Set a new path of enlightened redesign;
Never forget "Injustice anywhere is a threat to justice everywhere."
Treat every day like Juneteenth freedom is not far away,
We must pray, write and always convey;

That those days of bondage led to moral decay,
We cannot sit back in naïveté;
I will do my part to ignite, because "No weapon formed against me
shall prosper,"
I pray my brothers and sisters will concur!

Still Waiting for that Promissory Note!

On the anniversary of Johnson speech, let's take time to replay,
55 years ago today, Lyndon promised to fulfill rights and repay;
As an American with African descent, I have this story,
Still incomplete, it remains promissory;

All my life, I've felt this pain, don't know where it came from,
Causes tremors in the day, and sometimes makes me numb;
The doctors can't diagnose it, appears to dwell deep in my soul,
When activated, the sensation puts everything on hold;

Sometimes, it flares up, causing internal suffocation,
Reminds me of this generational lack of compensation;
The asphyxiation Eric Garner felt six years ago,
Was refreshed with George Floyd's breathless plea of woe;

I know you feel this helpless lack of control,
Waiting to exhale and regain your sense of whole;
But no matter how we try to achieve that golden ring,
There's a club, willing to cause a vicious sting;

Deprived of freedom, crippled by hate,
We strive with hands raised peacefully marching to eliminate;
Though we act with restraint, justice continues to be denied,
How many brothers and sisters have to die to be justified;

We can't breathe, when you attack our ability to vote,
That's not what the founding fathers, thought of when they wrote;
"We hold these truths to be self-evident, that all people are created equal,
Endowed by their creator, with unalienable rights" should be their sequel;

As a nation, convict us to live up to our credo,
We need amazing grace to overthrow;
The deceit that lies in the heart of man, has to be converted,
We shall never sleep or rest until injustice is subverted.

They Still Exist

As we commemorate the twentieth century prophet,
Never forget the pain of America's triple threat;
Militarism, poverty, and racism are still real,
Empowered layers of "privilege" refuse to conceal;

Unemployment may continue to spiral low,
but the humble beg for crumbs from the widow's tableau;
Hunger is ubiquitous on MLK Boulevard,
Less-than-standard etiquette one can't disregard;

Malnutrition causes brain damage that starts in the crib,
Need to eliminate food deserts with agricultural lib,
Gulf between well off and deprived widens by the second,
No nation is great until issues are reckoned;

Prejudice and bias philosophy is based on a contempt for life,
Arrogant assertions and absurd dogma ignite the fire of strife;
Racism is total estrangement, separating body, mind and spirit,
To say you love God and not neighbor makes one a hypocrite;

And what do we say of war, the ultimate destroyer that is not just,
Fills country with widows and orphans, it is our nation's disgust;
Injecting drugs of hate into veins of people normally humane,
Creates physically handicapped and psychological strain;

To fix these maladies take more than wisdom, justice and love,
It will once again take a nation, committed to help from above;
To alleviate the damage and the detrimental evil of these three,
Remember the words of the Master Teacher, who said
"If you do this to the least of these, you have also done it unto me."

A Father's Hope

I pray that my daughters are well,
That they mature and prosper as they excel;
I pray their lives are filled with meaning,
and Holy Spirit leaning;

I pray everything they touch turns to gold,
And God will bless them, ten, twenty even a hundredfold;
I pray their hearts will be at peace,
As they remember, they are each God's masterpiece!

A Father's Day Peace

As I muse in the library of the GTU,
I reminisce about all I've been through;
This place, its history, the books and volumes,
Speak to my spirit as I pass through
these hallowed rooms;

I'm grateful for the opportunity presented long ago,
To study, exegete passages in their authentic flow;
A debt of gratitude to mentors who shared,
They always ensured I was prepared;

This life-long student is still involved,
In getting human problems solved;
Church to prison, military to hospital settings
have been vehicles of support,
But deep in my soul
God has equipped me for another court;

Not anxious or concerned about this calling,
Yahweh will guide my steps for this Holy Spirit falling;
Thankful to Abba Father, that I still have the urge,
To listen and respond to this mystic dirge.

Time to Slow Down

No more alarm clocks, no more early rise,
No more staying in when you know it's getting late,
No more hurry up with sleepy eyes,
No more worrying about the traffic and the tailgate;

No more checking on the weather to see if it's cold or hot,
No more waiting for warm water to flow into the sink,
No more pondering if you left your badge, iPhone or what not;
No more wondering about lunch because you need water to drink;

No more sleeping on the bus hoping the next rider seats in the rear,
No more deadlines, emails and inter-office chat,
No more going to Dixon concerned about the fiscal year,
I'm sure you've found many ways to turn a stat;

To my twenty-year old friend who became my wife,
can't wait to see you rested and relaxed,

It's time to slow down, bash in the sunshine, enjoy life,
with a mojito in hand as you take a chill pill to the max.

Love Sonnet Number Seven

I do not love you like a cloudy sunset, that fades
into a forgettable horizon,
I love you like the tranquil blue inside the twilight,
when the pink glow passes through space,
scattering our hue in the atmosphere.

I love you like dew-kissed roses,
nurtured and trusted; perfumed
with sweet fragrance in perpetual bloom.

I love you without knowing the chilly dawn or
shadowy dust of tomorrow,
Time stops,
when your heart winks my smile widens,
igniting the wave of love
that began with volcanic urges.

Grasp my hand with all your fingers,
and touch the layers of petals inside our rosette,
The bright, waning sun approaches a memorable vista.

Waiting for our love to color the sky!

Reluctant Preacher

From the age of five God sent His Word,
tucked neat in a pocket over my heart.
Sacred expressions got me stirred,
Revelation knowledge did slowly impart.

Bible burned like coals would not depart,
couldn't sleep power transferred
predestined for purpose with heavenly support.

Family incident caused speech slur
in the natural, anxiety tried to abort;
Traveled eight thousand miles total deter
revelation knowledge did slowly impart.

Landscape in Letters

Looking
through viewfinder
writing visions of bliss
imagination captured wait
and see!

Double Double
A Cinquain

Ancestral Advice:
If I
could speak to him
I'd advise to take a
reflective pause, meditate use
wisdom

Note to Self:
Change is
very hard, it takes
discipline to alter
mental program and return to
basic.

Approved by God:
Within
the recesses of
the heart lays truth waiting
to be released, the warrior must
be freed.

Losing Control:
What if
the person you
paid is a con artist,
relations need trust to produce
quickly.

Never Thought:
Never
thought I would see
the day where LinkedIn meant
more than Facebook. The connections are
for life.

Journeys of the Heart

As I travel again on a journey of surprises,
I wonder how many will mask their disguises;
So many adventures and episodes,
Mysterious steps along this pedestrian railroad;

Some things never change in the rush from A to B,
A look to see who's safe another to see who's free;
This trip is reminiscence of the treks to Nairobi from Taveta,
Those long jaunts seemed to take forever;

People from every nationality fill these humble rows,
Who knows if this trip will resolve their emotional woes;
Is this the pinnacle for those who've traveled far
or is this a bleep on the traveler's radar;

Will the rider ever get just rewards for taking this arduous trip,
Or is this another exercise of genuine relationship;
I wish the one waiting could take a trip into the heart of the rider,
Then she might get a glimpse of the motive of this soul survivor;

Is a hug or a kiss all that one expects,
or should I presume more, from years of mutual connect;
I wish the passenger and hostess would finally understand,
It takes effort from both to make this journey truly grand!

The Cat's Meow

Just when I thought I'd lost that poetic spark,
your presence prompted a creative embark;
standing in the aisle pondering a purchase,
I was overwhelmed by your blushing face.

Your aura causes Milky Ways to shoot across my mind,
there goes another, catch a falling star design;
honey may not exemplify what I'm trying to avow,
there's no doubt you are the cat's meow.

When I call you Laura, infinity stands still,
as you sashay across the floor, Lord what a thrill;
never forget the power of heaven's touch,
to heal wounded hearts with a tender clutch.

Walking side by side, spirit beams,
hip to hip, two twigs strike fire, like a combustible dream;
I often wonder where you came from dimple peach,
from God's heart, glad you're never out of reach.

Awesome, distinctive, marvelous, great,
sensational, superb no doubt you're first-rate;
some may posture, like a fancy candlestick,
Your light is undeniable, because you're the lick!

The Jam of Friendship

The more I pour into this vat,
It entices me to contribute as we chat;
When I see sweetness from afar,
It draws me closer like the North Star;

Feet want to go in one direction,
But heart glides towards another reflection;
Eyes yearn to see sugar bundled off your neck,
Or flowing near the quarterdeck;

Either way doesn't matter,
Throw another strawberry into this bowl of chatter;
Will the smile leave with an image to post,
Or the eyes sparkle to reveal another dose;

You know what you're doing though it's been a long time,
I hope you don't think this friendship is a crime;
It's surreal how the jam forces us to cross each other's paths,
I would go crazy trying to do that math;

I think your life's better though you would never say,
Got enough pectin for both in this double play;
Friendship acquaintances call it what you will,
Thank you for the recognition it's your natural skill;

I never feel bruised by the gazing eyes,
Don't feel uptight in a pickle or slightly compromised;
I benefit from the presence as you skate across the floor,
Can't wait for the sweet concoction as we explore;

I know it's crazy there is no rhyme or reason,
Everything's appropriate in this sticky season;
One thing you know that will always be true,
Whatever happens I'll stick closer than glue!

What You Do for Me!

I may never know the depth of what you really feel,
But the percolation in my heart can't be concealed;
I realize how fortunate I am,
to receive messages by vibrational telegram;

Each thought brings rain from the Molokai Range,
If the sun doesn't rise, these promptings I would not exchange;
Primordial desires come from a deep subterranean place,
The thought of you transcends time and space;

I never met your father or shook his loving hand,
But somewhere in my spirit I feel his presence grand;
I sense you understand animals in an unusual way,
comprehending swans in their loving magical display;

You're Wonder Woman deserving more respect than Superman,
Your virtues of goodness makes anyone an instant fan;
I don't know why each morning a new flower enters my mind,
I wonder what the fragrance is I think it's called divine;

Wherever you go, whatever you do,
You'll always have a friend who'll pray you through;
You deserve the best of everything it's true,
So use wisdom in your next review!

All Because of Sophie

Don't know why I hesitated to call,
The impact you have is like a waterfall;
The excitement of your laughter the freedom of expression,
Takes my vagus nerve to a new direction;

Every phrase created is like the first time I heard you sigh,
I would be lying to myself if I do not cry;
I pray you find that special one that understands,
The depth of your spirit, the well you demand;

Tender, kind, considerate you know,
Inner outer attraction in a subtle ratio;
Who knew one person could excite,
The day and the night in just one flight;

Coast to coast seems so far,
But we share like neighbors who live next door;
Wheat grass lover thought I've never hear those words,
Who knew I'd get that close to a hummingbird;

May the healing angels touch Sophie's area of concern,
Pray the veterinarian's report is overturned;
This creature with humble eyes begs for attention,
Waiting patiently for a spiritual intervention!

But You Don't Hear Me
Conversations with Mom

Mom: How are you? I haven't heard from you? I didn't want to call too early, since I know you go to work.
Son: I called you five times, left messages on both phones! (Didn't respond to my comment).

Mom: I looked and deleted calls, didn't see your call. How are you? I was hesitant to call too early, because I know you are off on Fridays.
Son: You know I wake up before 6 am, you can never call too early. I've been trying to get you.
Mom: How have you been? Are you going away for Thanksgiving?

Son: No (lying because I wasn't sure what my elder sister had told my Mom).
Mom: it's not a good time to travel (fearful).

Son: Every day I leave the house, I have to be careful. I sent you a Thanksgiving Card.
Mom: Calling to see if Kayla's address is the same on Brooklyn Avenue.

Son: Yes, it's the same, she hasn't moved.
Mom: I know it's her birthday. I sent something to the older girl, earlier in the month. But I haven't heard anything from her, or her kids. Does she still live in the same town?

Son: Yes, Alecia still lives in McKinney.
Mom: I was thinking about sending some money for the kids for Christmas and let her purchase whatever she wants.

Son: Sounds good!
Mom: What are you doing for your birthday?
Son: Nothing!
Mom: Hard to do anything these days. Haven't heard from the insurance people about payment.

Son: (thinking Mom doesn't need to think about this because the issue is already resolved).

Mom: They say it's going to happen I guess. Will you drop by again, could you bring some lemons.
Son: (Interesting if she really wants lemons, my elder sister has more lemons on her tree then mine) Ok! (Knowing my lemons are not ripe yet!).

Son: Love you Mom!
Mom: You know I love you, you never have to doubt that.
Son: Love you Mom!

Psalm 106

Help us to
become true
bearers of

Joy, invite
us to the
cosmic dance

May we walk
by faith and
not by sight

Psalm 36

How precious
is your love
O kind God

In you is
the source of
life, and in

Your light, we
see hope, light
and glory!

Psalm 8

When I look
At the night
sky and see

The work of
your fingers
the moon and

stars set in
place, what are
mere mortals?

Like an Airball with a Prayer

Deep into that darkness dealing,
All my soul within me healing;
My teammate I could not awaken,
Dazed tired unmistaken;

So you came gently swishing,
All my soul within me dishing;
I threw my respect upon the floor,
Don't worry about me "mind the score,"

In there stepped a bruising pick,
Offense and defense took a lick,
No foul was called for either party,
The refs agreed this play was hearty,

So I screamed, "Is that an arc"?
You said, "clearly wide of the mark"!

Waimea Walking!

In the Valley of the Priests
I understood the signs,
as I took my time to get in line,
I slowly meandered down the road
parked near a bougainvillea grove,
When you slow your roll you can see
a bug, a leaf, or bruised reed,
The wonders of nature
are missed with too much speed;

With nothing on my plate,
I looked forward to these paths
that were curvy not straight;
Before entering I paused and stared,
Each square foot was a sacred prayer;

I looked to the right
was amazed by the sight,
Three story trees, manicured and spread,
I basked in the tapestry overhead;
The scenery was precious in every degree,
My camera too simple to capture nature's glee;

So I started up the shady path,
My favorites waiting for a visual bath;
My optic nerve feasted on
the wrinkles of each fruit,
I stayed long enough to give
each a spiritual tribute;

I passed the lily pads,
so peaceful and plain,
Noticed the flowers had closed
their petals waiting for more rain;
The ginger were abundantly seen,
Their placement auspicious and serene;

The lawn was green, broad
enough for a salutation,
Shadows of the canopy
made me leap in celebration;
The ivy growth covered the trunk,
and branches heading to the sky,
The elephant plants appeared
to listen to my lullaby;

So many downward steps
to descend,
I'd have to return to enjoy
each fluorescent bend;
It seemed like I was confused,
But each step created a new level of amuse;

As I approached the jewel of this place,
I felt God's embrace,
A calling to come closer,
for a heavenly smile;
As I viewed the waterfall from afar,
Others had tasted nectar from this jar;

Everything seemed peaceful, like Garden's eve,
So calm I dare not leave;
I pray when you take your next walk
make it special and plain,
**Listen closely to nature's message,
and you might receive a spiritual ordain!**

Jessie

Rome to Naples on the high-speed train,
Boarded in coach to keep travel plain;
Space big enough to occupy four,
As two we were tempted to lock the door.

Hope prayers were sent
as electric vessel left the station,
at last minute we accepted
a woman's invitation.

Fair, friendly Italian it seemed,
never considered her presence as a scheme;
Wife Susan wore New York
state-of-mind like a sign,
We lowered our guard never
expecting to be undermined.

During this 70-minute ride
we endeavored to engage,
To determine if Jessie
was sincere or onstage;
At no time did we look strange or hover,
as we pursued her character to discover.

Arriving in Naples at the Garibaldi station,
I went ahead to secure transportation;
Susan stayed behind to deal with her bags,
Jessie said, "She would help" possible red flags;

With luggage I walked and secured a ride,
waiting for wife to come alongside;
When I saw Susan, I knew something
was wrong,
tears filled her eyes like the caged bird song;

Surprised, it was the first time,
Spouse reacted at the scene of a crime;
She said, "The woman who
helped me cannot be found"
so Susan let out a primal sound;

"Jessie, Jessie" her name echoed throughout,
Filling the terminal with a fearful shout;
As we prayed a figure appeared through
the train's smoke,
Jessie's character spoke;
"I lost you Susan in the commotion,"
We may never know the true emotion;

We think though her thief-prone mind said abscond,
Her heart had created a different bond;
Lesson learned, no matter how a person seems,
Never allow any to divert your intuitive stream!

Old Road Trail

Can only imagine, stories shared on the Old Road Trail,
Blessed to meander and listen for pilgrim's tales;
Snake encounters of yellow and red,
Strange insects with furry legs, big heads;
Unique sage-like foliage of green,
Interesting endeavor to conjure up thicket scenes;
I'm sure you have a narrative of travail,
Grateful for God's grace that allowed us to prevail!

SEASONS OF THE HEART

Fireworks of the Heart

It only takes a spark to create the arc,
That curves the rainbow from heart to heart;
It only takes a minute to set the world aglow,
With the artistic flair of Picasso;
It only takes a second to set the record straight,
To reach across the aisle with harmony not hate;
Ignite the flame my citizens and friends,
And let's bring civility back to this nation again;
Vote!

NaiVasha's Song of Victory

Eight years before your birth,
Your name was spoken in your father's girth;
Carried your name in my spirit for years,
Through the heartaches, relationships and tears;

Wanted my first biological daughter to shine,
So I prayed for a name that was simply divine;
In the hot sun of Tucson you entered the world,
Precious glowing my "what a girl;"

Grew like a flower, beautiful and strong,
We continue to celebrate and lift up your song;
A song of triumph perseverance and desire,
A song of endurance through the rain and fire;

You've proven to yourself, 'whatever' can be done,
Through sleepless nights and little trites;
Declared through actions you have the "right stuff,"
Resilience, determination not easily rebuffed;

So we say gladly use wisdom in all that you do,
Pursue your dreams and always review;
The lessons you've learned in reaching this goal,
Channel all that energy with genius control;

There is no doubt you are gifted hope you never forget,
The prayers and the petitions of your spiritual cabinet;
Barbara, Kayla and Lee',
Grandmother and relatives stay on bended knee;

And every night before I lay down my head,
And rise in the morning to kneel by my bed;
Praying for a hedge of protection around your life,
That God would keep you safe among the strife;

So fly like an eagle above the storms and the rain,
And allow the love of God to sustain;
For the Good Shepherd will never leave, no matter where you go,
Keep climbing up the mountain as you reach each plateau.

Ode to Wheatgrass

To the Tune of "Do Lord"

Chorus
Wheatgrass, O wheatgrass, Ha! You are my friend,
Wheatgrass, O wheatgrass, my bud through thick and thin,
Wheatgrass, O wheatgrass, you're getting under my skin,
Way beyond the blue,

Verse One
I taped you to my elbows and taped you to my knees,
I put a small glass, over my eyes, n' the Sandman visited me,
I snorted a little up my nose and said, Whoa! thank you please.
Love all the benefits of you,

Chorus

Verse Two
Don't stop your healing virtues, to eliminate and clean,
I know with each new implant, my body feels supreme,
I've juiced so much wheatgrass, I'm a juicing machine,
Just the smell of you,

Chorus

Verse Three
Your taste is so delicious, your smell is "Oh, divine",
I can't wait to get back home, and drink you all the time,
So this is my story and wheatgrass is my dream,
Now, I'm clean and lean,

Chorus
I just love you wheatgrass,
I love the smell of you,
I love all the things you do,

You're a superfood,
You help digestion,
You lower cholesterol,
You lower blood pressure,

You even boost immune system,
I just love me some wheat grass,
Gives me energy,
It rejuvenates me
and I just feel refreshed,

O, I love me some wheat grass,
You're my friend, through thick and thin,
I love all the benefits that you,

You just keep on working,
On the inside, on the outside,
Grow some hair,
heal my diabetes,
stop the ringing in my ears

Thank you wheatgrass,
O, I love you,
and I'll just keep on drinking you
If you take care of wheatgrass,
wheatgrass will take care of you,

Hallelu!

What Does Sixty Mean
Ode for a Titan

From a biblical perspective,
very little as far as I can see,
For some this number means,
you've been married, once twice
or maybe even three;
It's about dinnertime in terms
of years on Earth,
A good time to reflect on
what our life is worth;
How do we measure our years
who sets the bar,
Is it determined by houses, cars
or how we've traveled afar?
Or is it decided by a different type of memoir?
In our own eyes, we're all rock stars;

I believe this precious
life is settled by how we treat each other,
Glad to see you Richard and Arlene,
my brother and sister from another mother;
Happy you made it this far through schools,
relationships, the toil and strife,
When I look back over the years,
I think we've had a wonderful life;
Because we've had some awesome moments,
some peachy and divine,
some groovy, startling and sublime;
But the beauty of this minute,
the miracle and wonder of what's fine,
is we made it with favor, this motley crew from Skyline.

So give your brother a high five,
Your sister a pat on the back,

Thank them for their friendship,
and understanding feedback;
We're together by the grace of God,
Grateful we can put away our facades;
Live in the moment, this sacred little time,
I'll cherish and keep it, like it's Christmastime;

I'll hold you up in prayer, for the things
you hold so dear,
This is my sonnet for the class of '71 year;
You'll always be my historical group and peers,
I hold you in my mind and soul,
Lift your cups and cheer;
We are the Titans, the mighty Titans,
Be blessed and thankful you made it to
This place, right here!

Eternally Always

What happens when you meet someone,
and your life is changed forevermore?
When the thought of that person,
changes the fiber, essence and
microorganism of your existence?

What do you do with all those emotions
that envelop your spirit,
That sends you floating into tomorrow
dancing into the nocturnal skies,
What do you do with the intensity
of that passion,
the fire in your belly?

These questions cannot be answered
within yourself,
They can only be answered within the
dialogue of the dance,
The sharing and caring,
     the listening and singing
          of hearts
       that bends toward the arc of truth,
If you find that one,
Tell them Today!

The Anointed Ira

When you play, the pianist of the past and
present accompany you,
When you play, I hear the symphony of Gershwin
and the melody of Beethoven,
The syncopation of Bach
and the resolution of Haydn,

When you play Scott Joplin walks to the piano
and puts his hand on your shoulders,
When you play Oscar Peterson is smiling
and Earl "Fatha" Hines is patting his foot,
The chords you strike compel our heart strings
to touch the flats and sharps of our life,

When you play I can see the chorus of piano players
and the choir of saints say in unison,
"It is well with my soul."

AUTUMN

Prayer for Autumn

"Keep your
heart with all vigilance,
for from it flow the springs of life."

Proverbs 4:23

I experienced a solar eclipse in Kenya, 1976.
Everything was effected by this phenomenon.
What would happen if we cared to look at
our hearts the way we desire to look at an
eclipse? At a time when the moral fiber of
our country is divided, we need an inner
eclipse of the heart. How you choose to
see defines the world you inhabit.

Today, I Cried Again

I should have cried with you on that dark rainy night,
Should have seen something in your spirit that wasn't right;

I should have sensed your monsoon of fears,
Should have been intuitive about our frontier;

I should have detected lightning in your soul,
Downcast eyes signified trouble in our hole;

I should have seen the tense confused missteps,
Felt the shallowness of this friendship depth;

I heard your thunder you never held it in,
Static charges hit like a whirlwind;

Fiery lady fueled with liquid acid,
Created my numb penchant for placid;

I cried again not with an external tear,
It was the start of an emotional drip that
keeps me present and aware.

Seasonal Change: Fall to Winter
Haikus

Bird of paradise
Speaks vibrance without a word
Wakes up primal roots

Yellow rose clusters
Grow tall, leaning towards light
Straighten up then wilt

White gardenia
Is this the last before frost?
Time has not yet come

Brownish leaves fallen
Alert eyes to season change
Inevitable

Orange leaf not sick
Lost chlorophyll, nature's trick
Plant going on pause

Citrus on trees ripen
Turning from green to yellow
From the inside out

If We Must Die, 100 years later

If we must die let us reverse each lie,
Bury claims that we are a craven race,
That caused us to sit instead of stand high,
Predestined to be content with disgrace;
Historians know the actual fact,
If we must die let the record reflect,
Let's not redact, misconstrue or distract;
We're bold people with keen intellect!
If insurrection is needed we know plot,
Remove structural racism to survive,
Retribute, for being caught, bought, and shot;
We know they will defend it with their lives;
Let Nat Turner's vision encase our soul,
Infuse us so we'll never be controlled!

I Will Not Be Triggered

Because death has slipped out of my hands,
Because I have seen the false hope of cancer,
Because I have heard the dreams of someone get better
only to get worse,
Because I have felt the stress of coronavirus,
Because I have lived in the red zone that exceeds safety,
I will not be triggered!

Because I have been depressed,
Because I have tried to medicate the pain,
Because I know what it's like to say it doesn't hurt
when it hurts so bad,
Because I do not have to hide anymore
and what a relief that is,
I will not be triggered!

Because I have heard the death gurgle in the room,
Because I have faced individuals with amputated limbs,
Because I have seen persons come into the
trauma room unresponsive,
Because I have seen a woman almost blow off her legs with a shotgun,
Because I have seen a man full of stab wounds.
I will not be triggered!

Because I have seen people die and come back to life
first with a pulse and then a heartbeat,
Because I have seen persons charged with the defibrillator
and not return to life,
Because I have had to witness tearful family members as
I shared their loved ones had passed away,
Because I have been sent to a room to give the last rites
as the angels gathered,
I will not be triggered!

Because I have felt the pain of marital infidelity,
Because I have felt the angst of my betrothed
crying like a baby,
Because I know what it feels like for someone
to not keep a promise,
I will not be triggered!

Because I know what it's like to cry for three years
because you can see the writing on the wall,
Because I know what it's like to hear your ex
tell you "I don't love you anymore,"
Because I know what it's like for your daughter
to stop talking to you,
Because I know what it's like to have arrows
pierce your heart,
I will not be triggered!

That does not mean that I cannot be affected,
That does not mean that I cannot cry,
That does not mean that I do not have compassion,
It means that I have a heart and I will pray for discernment,
I can hold others pain even as it is evoked in me,

I will not be triggered,
Because this pain has affected who I am and
with each breath I breathe through it all,
finding some semblance of peace,
Every day new techniques give me another chance to live,
Another chance to heal, another chance to restore
the broken synapses of my brain and heart strings,

I will not be triggered,
But I will remain steadfast,
Unmoved by catastrophes,
Unshaken by affliction,
Unstirred by devastation,
Holding trauma in my hands,

Fixed on the wellspring of love,
Rooted in the branch of hope,
Wrapped in compassionate care!

Just One Child, That's All I Ask

Just one child to hold so close,
just one child to touch their nose;
Just one child to embrace,
one child to see their face;
Just one child that's all she asks,
one child is this such a hard task;
Just one child to know you care,
this pain is impossible to bear;

Just one child I could deal with five,
but this sixth loss pregnancy I cannot survive;
So I quit, this is it, I can't take this tease,
You placed this little one in me, but then it leaves;
What kind of God is this so cruel, so mean,
This feeling I have makes me obscene;
My Dad told me, "Somebody prayed too much,"
I really can't understand people who say such;

This is really f-ed up, anger is driving me insane,
making me say thoughts that are profane;
Where are you, Divine One that I look to for grace,
Right now I need you to show Your face;
I could be on a beach drinking daiquiri and rum,
in Puerto Rico with my man in the sun;
But here I sit downtrodden and glum,
Where is the peace I need to overcome;

How will I make it, another day or fortnight,
Please Lord, help me through this plight;
Thank you, chaplain, you didn't move an inch,
you held your ground and didn't flinch;
Through all the tears, torment and grief;
You helped me scream it out and keep my belief;
Don't know how the days and months will transpire,
but I'm grateful you listened in my deepest mire!

Snake!

Careless walk filled with promise and delight,
Ashram tremors breathe celestial light;

Friends take steps to strengthen their soul,
Unaware booby traps wait on patrol;

It's often the adder's presence at bay,
Lurking in tension to leave or to stay;

Time determines the poison's real effect,
Just the thought of being bit brings neglect;

Didn't realize marriage was snake-bit fruit,
Who knows where to poke to extract the root;

Temporary masking a bandage fix,
Figuring out the truth a magic trick;

Careful when you enter this road of bliss,
Crooked places will be constantly amiss;

A serum must always be at-the-ready,
Capable to cure, heal and be steady!

Let Me Be the Sacrificial Lamb

Let me be the lamb that takes away the pain,
Let me be the lamb to fix "Me Too" shame,
Let me be the lamb blotted from the Book,
Let me be the lamb you never overlook;

Let me be the lamb not afraid to die,
Let me be the lamb holy purify;

Each time has a sacrificial lamb,
On one hill Abram fixed Isaac's jam;
Another hill the Lamb hung on a cross,
And bore the sins of humanity's loss;

The onus falls on this guard in the gap,
For men who've given women crap;
Ladies let not anger cause your veins to pop,
Get your arrows out and shoot your best shot;

Hit the lamb for the times you've been burned,
For mistreatment and calls never returned;
For dirt that turned your vibrant heart cold,
For unforeseen tales that may not be told;

Hit the lamb with belts that crushed your self-esteem,
No one should dismantle another's dreams;
For the razors that cut widespread,
The lamb needs to feel the anguish of dread;

Hit the lamb from the beginning to end
The lamb who caused you to descend;
The lamb warrants the pain of your grief,
With transference you'll get some relief;

Give the lamb your bitterness and contempt,
I'll take the mantle for the male attempt;
I hope when the lamb's penalty is paid,
You'll preserve with spiritual upgrade;
On higher ground I'll change our tune,
And usher in a redeemed platoon;
By putting the lamb around our necks,
We'll bring awareness to the quarterdeck;

When men incarnate the gift of this lamb,
Shed egos and the need for power scam,
We will with heart, level this playing field,
Get back to what it really means to heal.

Let me be the lamb not afraid to die,
Let me be the lamb holy purify!

My Humble Study Room

Walking gently into this humble space,
Desiring manna with each pensive pace;
Questions loom above my colorful mind,
Answers fall heavy quietly redesigned;

Inspiration springs from carpet below,
Vision shouts loudly in sharp stereo;
Black and white photo of past sacrifice,
Flanked by wifey hugs of pure paradise;

Cheerful flyer arrayed in green display,
Faithful church goer in Hawaiian lei;
Brown-toned Jesus adorned with eyes of fire,
Purviews dark thoughts with a purifier;

Lopsided ball caps protect head from rays,
Sweaty panama hats divert sunny days;
Bold black Stetsons is my secret weapon,
Teal-trimmed fedoras prevent half step-in;

Three-piece pinstripes distinctively matter,
Double-breasted never fails to flatter;
Navy dress blues make copy street-ready,
Tuxedo with patent shoes spell steady;

Worn red running shoes used to prime the pump,
Pace slowed by dingy green with Velcro hump;
Though gait is reduced wisdom shoots through slants,
Revealing fresh manna through prayer chants.

Eight by Ten by Seven

Like a skinny rat in a cement cage,
Time runs out to stay engaged;
Within the confines of this hole,
Fruitful endeavors develop my soul;

Stuck in prison bound far away,
Self-induced captive mental disarray;
Penned notes describing pics of pain,
Infrequent replies thought I was insane;

Red strain happens to a mind feeling trapped,
Cacti grows thorny trying to adapt;
Ancestry.com a likely place to start,
Family tree blooms within my heart;

Fiery urges flash like memories,
Evoking faith's calm guarantees;
Motherly smothering and Dad neglect,
Forced migration wandering to reflect;

No indoor plumbing or electric flow,
Was a reminder of times long ago;
Fetching water from a river to drink,
Revived grandma's tales of a filthy sink;

Unstuck emotions never felt alone,
Extremely comfortable in an African time zone;
Love life was modest learning how to chat,
Unforeseen bloating in this habitat;

Spicy micros went through me like water,
Changed to vegan diet post cow slaughter;
Meat eating ended that caused me to rage,
Became spiritual
like a skinny rat in a cement cage.

Sometimes I Get Tired

I get tired of conforming to
Eurocentric standards,
Tired of acting inauthentic
just to make others happy,
Tired of not feeling safe to live,
Tired of being monitored
by an overseer who feels
like a massa,

Tired of holding my peace
when I want to curse
the despot out,
Tired of blending to fit in
though I never liked
homogenized milk,

Tired of being treated like a black person
with a light complexion
as though my plight has been painless,
Tired of Du Bois "double-consciousness,"
looking at one's self through
the eyes of others,

Tired of running in place
when I want to leave the
colonizer in the dust,
Tired of being teacher/therapist
when white defensiveness
is triggered.

Tired of empathizing for others
when the other ignores my
existence,
Tired of not calling
a spade a spade,

Tired of smiling to not get shot,
Tired of demythologizing black people
for entertainment purposes only.

Tired of being choked by the smoke
of lies and deceit,
suffocated by toxic white fragility,
and an oil-laden rope
that is already on fire.

Tired of dominate culture asphyxiating our hopes
dreams and aspirations.

Tired of microaggressions, like
"You're so articulate,"
"Where are you really from?,"
"Why are you getting so angry?,"
"Your hair is so interesting."
"Can I touch it?"

Tired of dismantling the fact whiteness
is a 400-year-old invention,

Tired of being sliced-open
by the whip of neglect,
Tired of cheap grace
forgiveness without atonement.

Tired of praying for resilience and
acceptance to be Afrocentric,
Sometimes I get tired of the cost
of just being me.

John Gnat

I met a young fellow named John
who looked like an erratic gnat,
His head was shaved on the side
which made his eraser head flat;

As flat top bared his heart
he spoke of a God-sized hole,
He tried to fill it with junk
nothing satisfied his man-sized soul;

Apparent parental neglect
created a void,
A downward spiral caused this Vet
to be destroyed;

There are many avenues
when you feel deserted,
The only paths legitimate
are often perverted,

When you feel abandoned,
endless options attract attention,
Cuss a little, drink a little, even snort
to raise the tension;

These errant actions were really
not his strong suit,
Only facades and
carnal substitutes;

Some people need to be broken
to the rotten core,
Before they see and understand
the true score;

When he spit up blood
he finally saw the light,
If you don't correct your ways
it will end your flight;

He was hospitalized seven days to
get his life in shape,
That's the lifespan of a gnat
before their earthly escape;

On the seventh day, he hollered,
"Eureka" and the insight came on,
He realized his mission
and the reason he was named John;

Your purpose is to be the forerunner telling
others of good news,
Life's troubles can be reversed
when the Omnipotent resolves your blues!

Repulsamine

Hear ye, hear ye!
Get your daily dose of drugs right here,
People everywhere are taking repulsamine,
Works better than any drug in its class,
Boosts libido while lowering your immune system,
Doctors recommend it for increasing metabolism and
decreasing stress,

We repeat get your daily dose of repulsamine now,
Baby boomers are using repulsamine to lose weight,
lowers A1C and eliminates ABC,
Get it, get it, get it before it's gone!

Stop using at once if bones rattle, teeth chatter,
hands shake or breath stinks,
Lay down if ears bleed, stomach bloats,
nerves tremor, mouth drools or eyes bulge,
Call a doctor quickly if you have an allergic reaction,
develop a pelvic twitch or have an increase in bald spots.
If scarier symptoms develop, hang up
and call an ambulance immediately,
You're dying!

Crawling Out of The Pit
The Great Hoax

To my fairer brother you ought to be ashamed,
Of intentionally deceiving the world with false claims;

'Jesus is white' you professed though you knew the truth,
The Son of God was a brown-skinned Semitic
your attempt to hide this fact has been uncouth;

At a deeper level is a larger distortion,
Which has led to an ideological extortion;

Denying ancient black cultures their achievements,
Has caused generations of bereavement;

Your ploy to change the truth into a lie,
Must be stopped with a scholarly reply;

You have manipulated the Roulette table too long,
It's time to sing a revisionist song;

Crooked has warped Eurocentric mind,
That tried to erase Black African Spirituality by design;

This erasure is result of twisted white Christian thought,
Miseducation the wheel of this racist plot;

With con tools of excavation you dug,
Replacing positive boulders with a negative plug;

You replaced truth with fiction, affirmation with denial,
Clarity with distortion, the import of Afro-Asiatic culture still on trial;

Four hundred years you blasted a hole in Blackcentricity,
Filling this pit with misguided toxicity;

Each turn you misused the scholarly wheel,
Misquoted the brightest minds for convoluted appeal;

You discredited Sigmund Freud's claim,
That 'Moses was an African' as he proclaimed;

Will Durant defrauded his talent by lifting up Egyptian brain power,
To the detriment of Afro-Asiatic blackness he would sour;

Durant adopted a color-blind view to avoid the obvious fact,
Black cultural origins produced civilizations' greatest impact;

European and white American scholars engaged in a scheme,
'The Sumerian Problem/Question" to lower Afrocentric self-esteem;

A conspiracy to disguise Black ethnicity of the Sumerian clan,
This is known as the Great Hoax over a three century span;

Scholars dug a pit, asserting Mesopotamian-Sumerian culture over the
    Egyptian,
Not realizing the former, older culture had a black description;

Sir Henry Rawlinson's discovery shocked the academic world,
New data from cuneiform tablets caused minds to swirl;

Sumerians self-identified as, 'The Black-headed or Black-faced people',
This information destroyed ideas of white superiority laypeople;

With an anthropologist's scalpel, Dr. Don Matthews used an improved
    backhoe of restoration,
To repair the defective damage and make alterations;

With the skills of an investigative researcher,
Dr. Don debunked the distortions of the perpetrator;

Embracing Blackcentricity has become the method of study,
It must never be usurped as the understudy;

Matthews proved the Egyptians and Sumerians related to each other,
As students of sacred literature and culture let's treat them as brothers;

Like a surgeon cutting away cancer, Dr. Don removed a malignancy that
  has plagued academia,
Like a dentist removing an abscess, Matthews extraction has given truth
  voice as he cleaned the bacteria;

Like a chemist, this scientist created a litmus test that transforms the
  discussion,
Like a cardiologist doing a heart transplant, Dr. Don's research should
  resolve any faulty white racist repercussion;

Though outnumbered Matthews' certainty cuts like a sacred thread of hope,
His insights have changed Blackcentricity with a new scope!

Conflict of the Soul!

Is dark night of the soul the current norm?
Then how do we sojourn within a storm?

Can light be seen in tunnels of divide?
A battle lives between the wolves inside,

The minute feelings settle, lost resumes,
Disquieting purpose stuck in stagnant doom;

The choice of people interacting clear,
Impress some folks less, family time endear;

You have recurring dreams of former friends,
Opening self to love, to make amends;

Adverse disease are signs of life gone south,
Accentuate affliction's truth with mouth;

Discouraged spirit challenged to behave,
Accept the options given, alive, grave;

In silence secret wisdom yet concealed,
Deposits healing nuggets now revealed.

Listening Haiku

Don't be distracted
noisome pestilence, chaos
is all around you

God caused a strong wind
that broke rocks and an earthquake
and a fire happened

God's not in any
of that, but in His still voice.
I long for quiet

for His small voice to
be louder than all the noise.
To hush the noise of

the world so that His
whispers might be the single
echo in my heart.

The Weathered Cup

This piece of metallic is my savior. It has enhanced my life more than once. Since I started preaching forty years ago, the liquid that flows from this silver vessel is sweet. Because it's reliable, I'll call it "Old Faithful."

When people want to give me a cold drink of water, my protective cup raises up barking like a doberman pinscher and instantly morphs into a fire-breathing dragon and speaks in a baritone voice, asking the cold water bearer, "How dare you bring my master cool water, knowing your offering will destroy his speaking gift? Be gone, before I smoke your ass with flames of insult!"

My ubiquitous cup has traveled through time providing poetic comfort to those who are receptive. This cup was present when David the shepherd, spoke in Psalm 23rd of it running over. This cup showed up at The Last Supper as a vessel for the wine, passed amongst the disciples. Jesus the Good Shepherd, spoke of this cup in the Garden of Gethsemane as he surrendered to God's purpose for his life, "Take this cup away from Me, nevertheless, not what I will, but what You will."

This celebrative cup was at my parents' wedding in 1946 as Dad toasted joyously with his older and younger sister, Bea and Zemma, the woman of his dreams Juanita— my mother. A soot-covered replica of this cup almost melted in the Louisiana fire, when the Ku Klux Klan torched my parents' house. They thought my light-skinned father had broken the anti-miscegenation laws by marrying my dark-skinned mother. A beat-up cup showed up as a talking piece in Mississippi as Dad sat around the table discussing voting registration strategy with Martin Luther King, Jr. in 1960.

Later in 1963, this observant cup sat in the kitchen and watched my father beat my sister with sixty lashes from a skinny black belt. That same gossip-oriented cup laughed as I got whipped for telling my friends about my sister's misfortune.

Yes, Old Faithful has been there, through the good times and the bad, the wind and the rain, and all the frustrating pain. It chuckled when I stole Southern Comfort whiskey from my parents' stash, "My God-fearing father didn't need it anyway." This cup mischievously smiled, when I brought a woman home for the one and only time while my parents were away.

When I went to Africa, this lonely, deprived cup showed up on my table with no lights and no electricity. I wonder how Old Faithful survived those dark days and lonely nights. As I hiked, this cup appeared soaking up the rays from Mt. Kilimanjaro. I almost used this cup as a weapon when a bat slept next to me on a sisal bed. Didn't want Old Faithful to experience bad dreams, so I used a garbage can instead.

To remove it from harm's way, I have given Old Faithful, the highest honor imaginable, by naming it Emeritus. Can't throw it away, because I don't want it to destroy any marine life, or get wrapped around some dolphin's tail. It now sits within hand's reach, with my best writing utensils. My favorite highlighters, multi-colored pens, mechanical pencils, scissors and staple fill this cup with memories. It has paid its dues and fought the good fight. Now if you don't treat Old Faithful with respect, you might find yourself in one of my poems as a satirical joke.

Yes, Old Faithful is my savior and this silver cup, small at the bottom and large at the top, can seat and lounge on my mouse pad any time of the day or night. If I'm lucky, this weathered cup will have a pow-wow with my other desktop friends and narrate some juicy stories.

The Steps of a Good Man
Ballad for Eugene Goodman

Chorus
Goodman, Oh, Goodman
We will sing your praise,
Goodman, Oh, Goodman
True valor was displayed
Goodman, Oh, Goodman,
Mob led another way,
Your actions saved the day!

Verse One
On a winter chaos morning
Man-of-honor made a move
Employed usual wit as a mindful harpoon,
Diverted angry persons with something to prove,
Way beyond the blue,

Chorus

Verse Two
Using his body, as a human shield,
He-became the rabbit to their wolf pack zeal,
Leading them away from chambers
on Cap-i-tol's battlefield,
Way beyond the blue,

Chorus

Verse Three
Combat hero, long before that day,
DC's Native Son, values did not sway,
When asked about his actions, sighed,
I'd "do the same thing again" today,
Way beyond the blue,

Chorus

Verse Four
We feel safe, with peace as we see,
You escort Kamala Harris our historic VP
keep standing as protector
Against all enemies, we decree
Way beyond the blue,

Chorus
Goodman, Oh, Goodman
We will sing your praise,
Goodman, Oh, Goodman
True valor was displayed
Goodman, Oh, Goodman,
Mob led another way,
Your actions saved the day!

A Word of Caution Ojisan

I don't mean to make
generalizations,
But Uncle Ojisan
Your demeanor is disgusting,

How do you fathom standing
in front of the television,
Knowing that you are blocking
others from view,

I used to hesitate speaking
about these subtle biases,
but you have taken my angst
to bullhorn level,

You came into this place of business,
assuming you could bogard an
appointment because of who you are.

Elder, senior, Japanese hierarchy,
expecting to get special service,
There is no excuse for your
bullying behavior.

You didn't have a scheduled
time and it appears you didn't want
to wait two hours to be seen,
by the person who helps;

Entitled who are you to walk
over people, as if they are not there,
How did you develop this myopic perspective,
that you are the privileged one
to enjoy the fruits of society,
by tough guy tactics?

Was that superiority complex
acquired as you invaded
sister lands in WWII,
or did low self-esteem develop as you
looked to Americans for emulation?

This would not be so bad,
if this was an occasional mishap,
But after I left the medical office
your kind exhibited disrespect again.

As I looked for a food selection,
your brother pushed me before I decided,
didn't you see I wasn't finished,
but this is the second time in thirty minutes.

You've ignited my Nat Turner nerve,
and I'm ready for another Battle of the Midway
because you will not treat me like the
invisible man,

It's not my fault, you were on the
losing side of the global war,
I know that must have been humiliating
because you put emphasis on shame.

Your collective loss seventy-five years ago,
is no reason to belittle me.

Don't blame me, for being interned
in concentration camps for three years,
while I, your African brother was placed in
feces-infested ship dungeons for four hundred.

I know I will never be seen as your equal
though I visit your country, you treat me
like a zoo animal with the tourist in the cage,

How dare you think you've paid your dues
to one up anybody, because of your ethnicity,
you need cognitive behavioral therapy,
in how to treat other people of color.

Yes, I am speaking to you Uncle Ojisan
my Japanese brother,
Twice in one day, is twice too much;
I cannot keep quiet about this any longer,
Your actions stink to 7th heaven.

This is my prayer of forgiveness,
because reconciliation may not be possible,
If black lives don't matter,
If you deny responsibility for your actions
or do not admit you've hurt me.

I forgive you for killing me with your
arrows of disdain,
For stealing the positive aspects of my heritage
and turning them to lift up your own,
For lying and hiding with implicit bias your true feelings.

Unless you change,
and treat me with honor and respect
You will never reach enlightenment
Bad karma will follow,
and you are doomed to repeat
the cycle of rebirth again and again!

The Pressed Shirt

I am a pressed shirt.

I am not the shirt
you buy in the store
with straight pins at every crease
cardboard in the collar
to maintain the frame
with chiffon paper
that gives a soft look.

I am not that perfect.

I am a pressed shirt,
preferably laundered
at the cleaners.
Fresh fragranced
with medium starch.

I am a pressed shirt
dressed for success
because the
next first impression
could change my life.

My pressed shirt persona
has ancestral roots.
Mulatto grandfather
known as "Uncle Bud"
was barred from literacy,
pressed clothes
for thirty years.

Suave tall Uncle Bud chose to press
cloth created from cotton
rather than pick it,

His scarred-hands and aching back
had paid the price,
of long hours in the lime-enriched
loam of Louisiana.

Parents used picking
cotton as prerequisite
for rite of passage.
"Son, you don't
know hard labor until
you're worked all day
in the cotton fields."

As I perused my Dad's closet
pressed white shirts were aplenty,
I hoped my closet would be
equally adored.
I was never informed of
the consequences of
wearing the pressed shirt.

Every black man that wears
the pressed shirt
is not only rated individually,
their performance is rated against
every black person that
has ever lived.
That seems crude
but it is reality.

Dad's shirt collection
was distinguished by
collar types
mostly classic collars.
Exclusively
white
simple, plain

angles pointing down
with french cuffs
for formality.

The jewel of this collection
was a
mandarin collar
black
complex, extraordinary
with a three-inch
white clergy attachment.

This was the creme de la creme
of the pressed shirt.
It represented instant
respect, honor, courage.
While no one looked
at the white pressed shirt
when it entered the room,
conversely eyes rolled,
necks flexed in all directions,
when the black pressed shirt
with white high collar
walked into the room.

This pressed shirt exemplifies
I've done hard labor in the
battlefield of life.
Clean fit body
plant-based
hydrated, sleep-nurtured
operationally ready to be present.

This pressed shirt represents
the tapestry of my legacy.
Over hundred years of
indentured service.

If you stand close you can
smell the grime of the cotton fields,
see the dirt around my neck,
the wrinkles on the back,
If you study long,
you might see a tear stain from
listening to a wounded warrior.

Though I wear the white
pressed shirt,
it is perfunctory.
I work twice as hard
in the black pressed shirt
because by wearing it
I get instant access to the hospital,
courthouse, crime scene
and prison.

When this earthly battle is over
and my war-torn body is laid to rest,
you may not remember the smile on my face
the position of my hands
or how I made you feel,
but you will remember my pressed shirt.

Black Man's Prayer for Forgiveness
Dramatic Monologue

With hands covering my face and
eyes glazed downward,
I come on bended knee to plea for
the collective wrongs of our black brethren.

For too long we have shuffled our feet
Numb, drunk, confused
and cleared our throats speechless,
Fearful of embracing the violence imposed on our Nubian Queens.

You have every right to be bitter, enraged
for we have talked out of our necks,
and shirked our responsibility to protect
you from the colonizers.

Forgive us for putting on the armor of the oppressor,
For the dirty pain we have spewed
through fight, flight or freeze response,
No excuse for our abuse.

Forgive us when we have talked but not listened,
For denying your lived experience,
For demeaning your existence
By objectification, avoidance or denial.

Forgive the unintentional fragmented pain
of 400 years that oozes from our pores,
At times we sweat self-hate through lies to cope
No excuse for our abuse.

We are not ignorant of divide and conquer strategy
that entices us daily with dissent against family.
We are united in the systemic racist disdain,
but you deserve integrity through clean pain.

Time to rewrite the script,
scratch the derogatory comments,
setoff a revolution that heals,
by creating a redemptive renaissance,

A period that causes black men to stand,
An era that accentuates we understand;
For we can never be real men, until we cherish our sisters,
embraced and valued as dynamic co-creators;

I will do my part, by holding other men accountable,
If we are complicit, we condone the pain to our sisters
When we disrespect women, we disrespect ourselves,
Somebody's got to man up,
Think before you speak, honor every word
With prayer, we can make breakthroughs.
change and restore history with positive reviews;

When gratitude is appreciated,
Happiness will flow,
Through dialogue, we'll become allies,
Friends, partners, hand in hand, eyes toward the sky
As your Nubian King,
I will be King T'challa, with you, my Queen Nakia
We'll reign with adoration, love and peace
Wakanda Forever!

Just Be Frank

Dedicated to Chaplain Frank, VA Sacramento

Adjustment tension and stress hovers in the air, as he
Bears witness to the physical pain of patients, needing
Compassionate care both horizontally and vertically.
Dedication drips from first responders, helping him to
Establish algorithms of care. Religious survey reveals
Faith is the common denominator that lifts, the care-
Giver and guides them to decompress, providing
Health and healing, and respite to inhale hope.
Initial assessment of needs, alerts chaplain when to
Juxtapose output versus stress for staff, patients and family.
Keeping documentation aids interdisciplinary team, assisting
Life review of beliefs, values and practices.
Ministry of presence increases by listening to their stories,
Offering spiritual care through prayer, sacraments, triaging
Proactive versus reactive needs of care, strategizing
Risk monitoring, ensuring the discipline of
Spirituality is the belief that a Higher Power is in control.
Turning trials into triumphs is a ministry goal.
Understanding the grief and loss experience,
Visiting and facilitating emergent concerns allowing the
Work of the Holy Spirit to guide him authentically, not like a
Xeroxed copy of who he wishes to be. This is his moment.
Yielded to the leadership both above and on Earth,
Zealous for the healing power of God for such a time as this.

Prayer for Veteran's Day

Today, we bow to honor the service of Veterans,
Those who stepped up to the plate to follow God's plan;
For the valor and courage, commitment and zeal,
We honor your heart and patriotic ideal;

Words of thanks may never repay,
The blood, sweat and tears you exhibit each day;
But we pause as a nation to give you props,
We will never forget your service as the cream of the crop;

Let us honor you not only by our word,
But by giving an ear for you to be heard;
Let each recommit our lives, to the service of the heart,
To a form of giving we can all take part!

Women Tricube

Female Vet
Hospital
Needing test

Outsmarting
Breast cancer
Appears clear

With new way
Cat poking
Pray answered

Advent Tricubes

Light and Shadow
Isaiah 9:2

The people
who walk in
darkness will

see a great
Light. For those
who live in

a land of
deep darkness
light will shine.

•

God with Us
Matthew 1:23

May the Light
that entered
the world that

night cast its
brilliance
into the

deepest seam
of our souls
peace on Earth.

•

Resilience

Do not wait until
Conditions are perfect, new
start builds the ideal

A Thousand Sunsets

I wish I had a thousand sunsets, that I could visit day to day,
A time to look at God's majesty as I walk along the way;

A time to realize this moment has occurred so many times,
I wonder and ponder, it boggles the human mind.

The shadows of the mountains, the curve of every hill,
Is magnified a thousand times when viewed from God's windowsill.

It makes Psalm Twenty-Four come to life,
"The earth is the Lord's, and all its fullness,
the world and those who dwell therein,"
Wish I had a thousand sunsets so this poem would never end.

But all I have is this one sunset to visualize and enjoy,
To appreciate the splendor that is set before.

A sunset for me, a sunset for you,
This sunset lives in my heart a thousand times to view.

An Auntie for the Ages

Amazing Auntie was always present with
Blessings of concern, giving guidance to
Children, was her passion, regardless of kin.
Dedicated to the young, gifted and black,
Empathy was her tablecloth from which,
Fresh fruits of kindness, courage, commitment,
Gratitude was served. Each Thanksgiving,
Hospitality flowed with peace, and love, as we
Interceded for those needing deliverance. The
Joy of the Lord was complimented with creative
Know-how from artists, musicians and writers. She
Loved them all from Gwendolyn Brooks and Claude

McKay, to Georgia Johnson, Bessie Smith, Nora
Neale Hurston. Her life was a walking repository of
Orations. She could recite "The Creation" like a
Prayer, and found positive ways to combat
Racism, through mentoring, and being a
Sojourner of life, waiting for heaven's reward.
Take a page, from my auntie's postscript.
Unity was her motto, bringing harmony to light
Victory her credo, through trials and strife,
With mercy on her left, and goodness on her right,
Xerox was the opposite of her originality
Yielded to the spirit, led by the Word, Aunt
Zemma will live on in our heart for the Ages!

Humble Yourself

Humble yourself
to the crystal bead
of perfect humility,
No matter how holy
you advance,
One can never
be free of
blind spots.

Humble yourself
prostrate your heart
to the blade of grass,
See ego shrivel
in the ground crust
of dry-burnt moss,
and you will find
the seed.

Humble yourself
to the stream
that flows
to the ocean,
Lay flat
and you will
find humility that
gives the
ocean power.

Humble yourself
Press in naked
without old garments,
be useful
show your
vulnerability.

Humble yourself
to the way of the leper,
be human like Naaman
go wash seven times
in the dirty, Jordan River.
At the moment of openness remove all debris,
let this virtue shine
in the pearl of true humility!

Brother Jerry, How I Long to See Your Face
Elegy for Jerry Wade

My brother from another mother,
How I long to see your face,
To take you to the mountains
even to the mall,
To walk along the seashore
or view the waterfall;

I want to spend a little time
and heed some Godly advice,
Anything from your wise heart
tried in the fire of sacrifice;
I want to discuss how military
service impacted your decisions,
Did it help your dreams and daily visions?

Appreciate your family
you raised some awesome sons,
Their grit is admired by everyone;
Rest assured if they ever need a hand
or shoulder to rest their head,
They can always visit our abode
as a watershed;

Brother Jerry I might need your angelic help
once and a while,
Please glance down upon my actions
as I run this gospel mile;
Just some guidance along the pilgrim journey,
Help me brother as I trust and obey;

Since you've gone ahead save a place
along the streets of gold,
I heard it's mighty glorious

at least that's what I've been told;
Will miss your jovial spirit
and your infectious smile,
You made every moment,
precious and worthwhile;

Every morning and every day
as I receive a little grace,
I look forward to that day
when we meet again
face to face.

Mother, Mentor, Member
Elegy for Fannie Jeffrey

As mother, I witnessed her daughters and sons in school,
They appeared to stick to the Golden Rule;
Their character and disposition seemed so real,
Their commitment and courage would often reveal;
Fannie's motherly touch and freedom to speak,
I wondered what made them so unique;

The curiosity of those early years in nineteen sixty-eight,
Slowly made sense on Outlook at the party gate;
Always organized decent and sometimes late,
Felt obligated to stay after, clean up and appreciate;

What a privilege to meet a Mom who truly understood,
That young people need a place to develop their neighborhood;
What a blessing to tell my Mom, "I'm heading to Outlook Way"
and she would yell back without thinking, "OK;"
Oh, if we had more mothers like Fannie,
Growing up wouldn't seem so awkward and uncanny;

But not only was Fannie a mother, she served as a mentor for others,
When we needed direction in a path,
She would give us ten options and observe the aftermath;
Always concerned about our direction,
No matter how far we fell, she advised us to rise up like a resurrection.

But of all the roles that I was privileged to view,
None impacted more than Fannie's membership in the church pew;
As her pastor for six years she never complained,
Though she was tired, sore and physically drained;
She gave me hope as I proclaimed good news to the merciful,
I knew she was grateful.

So I sing because I'm happy, I sing because Fannie's free,
Her eyes were on the sparrow, and this is the Lord's guarantee;
There's a place for Mother Jeffrey, a place not made with human hands,
A place among the angels and the heavenly Everglades;
You fought the good fight among us, you showed us how to discourse,
Now is laid up for you a crown precious and beauteous;

Watch over us Mother Jeffrey with heavenly guidance, we know you will,
We'll never forget your earthly presence that helped us to be still;
And when we look at the horizon or way up in the sky,
Just drop a falling star our way to graciously signify;
We loved you as a Mother, some even as a mentor too,
But God loved you so much, He said time to join the heavenly crew!

Friends Like You!

What a joy it is to awaken to friends like you,
People with heart who are there to see me through;
Friends that send roses wrapped in written vases,
Others that send lyrics with loving graces;
How fortunate I am to look into your faces,
To hear your rallying cry from yonder places.

I feel the sun of your friendship on my head,
I sense your celestial presence as I eat my bread;
The power of your warmth is so widespread,
Your kindness flows from our communal riverbed;
Heart to heart we're connected by this red thread,
Of hope peace and love from the Godhead.

I do not know how I got so blessed,
To be nourished by the kings and queens of God's gentleness;
I guess the angels and ancestors agreed,
It was time to drop some pineapple rain on a soldier in need;
I truly hope when you need a friend to walk beside,
You will not hesitate to let me listen to your insides;

Because where would we be, if it wasn't for our touch,
A hand, an ear, a hug, that means so much;
Let us remember the power we possess,
The influence to alleviate one drop of stress;
It may not come by telephone or text reply,
Just remain eternally as the apple of my eye!

Ode to Janvie

If I were a botanist:

I would create a flower called Janvie,
A fragrant rose to be grown
as a bonsai or a tree;
When you inhale
I see the ocean
cover the footprints in the sand,
When you exhale
I feel the breeze
in the weeping willow stand;

When you smile
the clouds move to reveal the sun,
When you blink,
eagles soar for a landscape run;

Thank God for your existence
your breath and heart,
So glad your spirit lifts every
vessel for a higher impart.

A Time for Every Season

Marriage can be hard sometimes.
Even the best marriages have
seasons of difficulty,
But this felt like the final act.
All of the signs of desperation
pointed to the fact.

Sitting on the shiny oak staircase
looking out of the curtains,
I could see a dull tree
with no fruit on its branches,

No pine cone waited for the wind,
no acorn suspended in space,
deciding to stay on the limb or
descend to the ground,
not even a dead rotten walnut
could be found.

This tree was bare.

The winter has taken every
exoskeleton
from the branches,
leaving it exposed and naked,
like a snail without a shell.

This February was more than the
middle of winter,
it was the beginning of a season
of marital cold winds and
frigid emotional turmoil.
Marriage is like a tree.

Marriage is connected to the root structure,
created by families coming together
to become one.
Often when a hybrid is grafted
on the structure of a different type of tree,
problems occur.

Inter-racial marriage is like an orchid
attached to a tree, that does not
penetrate the bark.
Two people from different cultures,
different values, different views
desiring to grow as one.

Marriage can be hard sometimes.

Tokenism Blues

Blackbird, sing a song of your flight,
Lost in this cold, white light;

Drowning like pepper in the salt,
conflicted like crack in the fault;
I fell into the Anglo hole,
naively shy without control.

Gasping for air in this journey,
Racism's chokehold warranted a gurney;
Red eyes stared with much delusion,
yearning to quiet this confusion.

Blackbird, sing a song of your flight,
Weaving in this hot, black night;

Reached for weed to medicate,
It caused me to denigrate;
Pondered, am I the only one?
No better than any native son;

Felt social stress, if I slipped up,
Prayed, "Please remove this bitter cup;"
If I made a mistake, I feared
I'd set black folks back a hundred years;

Blackbird, sing a song of your flight,
What will be my lasting plight?

Paid dues for others to succeed,
Suffered through grief and misdeeds;
Would repeat, through assault and strife,
It's the shrapnel I wear for this token life.

A Poet is Not...

A poet is not a vapor
that appears for a little time,
and then vanishes away.
A poet is like a whirlwind that whistles,
with pressure waves through our brain,
predicting a storm is coming.

A poet is not a spark plug
with dry, sooty deposits
that causes the engine to
misfire when the key is turned.
A poet is like a fine-tuned
Ferrari, that fires smoothly on
all twelve cylinders, giving it
a resonant sound of pure joy,
borne from world-class engineering.

A poet is not a rock
that remains eroding over eons;
a poet is like a watery brook that
washes over bedrock sending forth fresh
restorative energy into
the arteries of human existence.

A poet is not a piece of wood
cut by a serrated blade;
a poet is like a tree,
rooted in the earth, that continues to flower and bloom,
growing deeper and higher with each taproot
providing seed for future growth.

When these elements of air, fire, water and earth
are guided by the spirit, you cannot negate
their poetic force.

This dynamo resonates like the human anatomy,
That walks with the whirlwind of Phillis Wheatley,
stands with the dynamic courage of Paul Dunbar,
enveloped by the protective arms of Langston Hughes,
strengthened by the shoulders of Nikki Giovanni,
uplifted by the back of Dudley Randall,
and the constant heartbeat of Maya Angelou.

When these truths are manifested
nothing can stop the creative flow,
Not wind, nor fire,
water or earth;
for the poet is a prophet,
who speaks divine inspiration
reverberating into the hearts of generations,

Free at last, Free at last,
With love and grace
The poet sets us,
Free at Last!

Fragile: Handle With Care
Haikus

Dandelion puffs
plant seeds in spiderweb strong
message from spirit

Butterfly wings sit
on fortune cookie with note;
old crush will come back

Orchid brooch reminds
wearer: give bouquet of roses
while you are living

Delicate earrings
symbolize hot lunar nights
with sheer black stockings

Love letter biscuits
dripping with homemade jelly
trust is being served

Heart shaped clouds sprinkle
silver hopes of dreams deferred,
let the silence speak

These are the fragile
scenes of her soul that wait for
a gentle hand touch.

EPILOGUE

Recently, I was honored to have one of my fellow colleagues in our CLI class write a poem dedicated to me. I am just as excited about this offering as I was for the first poem written for me in 2012, in fact even more so, because it is confirmation that my meaning and purpose continues to inspire the next generation.

Jerome's Praise

I'd be lying if I said everything was going great
But I smile because I live to see another day
I'd be joking if I said that everything was going fine
But I'm grateful because I know that life is my design
I take what I am given and work to make it best
I am thankful to recognize that I've been blessed
I know I'm being protected ancestors above
I feel generations of their unconditional love
I hold my head high and prevail through the night
For the next day will be such a beautiful sight

—Aiyana Da'Briel

Poem for Mr. Thomas

What I witnessed, I can't believe my eye,
A truly majestic creature has fallen from the sky;
Never in my days did I anticipate such a teacher,
In this Greek speaking, Kenyan teaching, God-fearing preacher.

I have seen a lot of subs after many a sun and moon,
From timid Mr. Lionheardt, to Mr. Carl C. K. Koon,
I love Mr. Merrill, his respect goes off the grid,
But I have never heard him correctly pronounce the Hebrew name Abed.
Yes this man is something special, his style is very stellar,
Whenever he puts pen to paper, he writes a New York Best Seller,
When he's not spinning gold, he moonlights at San Quentin,
It's rumored that he even converted Charles Manson into a Christian.

He likes writing poetry, goes to high schools and begins to rhyme,
Has more flow than Easy E, Eminem & Dr. Dre combined,
This man is a legend, no sub is quite the same,
So I really cannot believe that no one knows his name.

—John Luke Bruni
Student, Rodriguez High School, 12/3/12

ACKNOWLEDGMENTS

I want to thank life-long friend Rev. Dr. Don Matthews, who has been an encourager with his articulate books and publications of truth since our years in seminary. Though we lost touch temporarily, we reconnected in time to empower us through major literary projects. This is my promise to him and a testimony to our friendship. Moreover, I would like to thank Rev. Dr. Floyd Bland, who has encouraged me over the past thirty years with his own list of books, and weekly inspirational texts. So glad Floyd moved back to California.

From a work perspective, my principal encourager has been my Webmaster and friend, Nasstassia Sitze. As an acclaimed spoken word contributor and artist, she has critiqued my poetry, photography and videos for over a year. Her honesty and feedback has made this process rewarding.